FAITH BURNING WITH HOPE

FAITH BURNING WITH HOPE

A Catholic Layman Wrestles With His Church

THOMAS W. MAHAN , KSG, PHD, HUMD

Library of Congress Control Number:		2011963011
ISBN:	Hardcover	978-1-4691-4057-5
	Softcover	978-1-4691-4056-8
	Ebook	978-1-4691-4058-2

This book was printed in the United States of America.

To order additional copies of this book, contact:
Xlibris Corporation
1-888-795-4274
www.Xlibris.com
Orders@Xlibris.com
101157

CONTENTS

Faith does not quench desire; it inflames it.

—St. Thomas Aquinas

With profound respect and deep love, I dedicate this book to the following:

Susan Petersen, my wife, whose presence is a constant
reminder of God's generous love.
My children, Maureen Mahan Copelof and Thomas Brendan Mahan,
Who are a joy and proof to me that the world is charged with God's grandeur.
My sister Carol, the only saint in the Mahan family and my faithful cheerleader.

Fear is the beginning of despair even as hope is the beginning of daring.

—Thomas Aquinas

ACKNOWLEDGEMENTS

I OWE MANY PEOPLE a tremendous debt of gratitude because they have given me the courage and the support to pen these pages. I love the Catholic Church and am grateful for the guidance and grace with which it has showered me. I am especially in debt to, and fond of, the church communities that have been a home for me and a source of inspiration. I list below some of the many from whom I have received gifts beyond measure. Probably none of them will or—in the case of the deceased—would agree with all that is included in these pages. Nonetheless, they have been an important influence on my evolution, on my struggle to discover myself and thus the meaning of my faith and my church. It has not been easy for me to throw away the masks or tear off the fig leaves that I thought made me acceptable. I know that I have not been totally successful in facing myself naked and probably even less successful in facing the world naked. But to the extent that I am open, honest, and free to accept my vulnerability and my frailties, the persons listed below have helped that come to be.

First, I must mention my father, Thomas W. Mahan Sr., and my mother, Agnes Sullivan Mahan, both remarkable in their talents and their generosity. They provided me with a sense of belonging, of being loved, and of a world that I could depend upon, which I am confident, gave me the talent to find joy even in the midst of pain. My three wives, Marie Schaefer (deceased), Aline Mattson (also deceased), and Susan Petersen have continued to reinforce and enhance that gift from my parents for almost sixty years. Each of them has been/is a joy who continues to create joy in my life.

My children, Maureen Mahan Copelof and Thomas Brendan Mahan, are marvelous creatures who for me are evidence of the great goodness of our God—Creator, Teacher/Savior, Companion/Advocate. Whenever I have doubts about the world, I turn my thoughts to them and to my wife Susan to reignite my enthusiasm for life. My two sisters have played a critical role as well. Ardie (her real name was Agnes) has been dead for over thirty years. My sister Carol, the saint in the family who was widowed over a quarter of a century ago, is now a legally blind pillar of the church.

They both were accepting and supportive as I struggled to become free, unencumbered by masks and fig leaves.

My spiritual life has had many wonderful mentors, guides, and associates. Monsignor Joseph M. Griffin, PA, became a spiritual father to me in my first four seminary years and continued to be a wise counselor. Sister Mary Gabriella of the Sisters of Saint Joseph was a spiritual mother, a woman of great faith and great caring. Both of those very influential persons are long deceased, but are vividly alive in my memory. The Most Reverend David B. Thompson, retired bishop of Charleston, is a giant in the later days of my evolution. Though only a few years older than I, he had wisdom and talent far beyond mine, and he gave me opportunities to grow and accolades far beyond my deserving. He trusted me, and I hope that I have proved trustworthy. Another significant person in my development over the past thirty years was the late Right Reverend Abbot Francis Kline, OCSO. Abbot Francis consoled me in pain, challenged me in my thoughts and actions, and provided a model for me to marvel at. Another important figure was Sam R. Miglarese, STD, with whom I still enjoy a comradeship and a closeness.

My pastor, Father Carl T. DelGiudice, has for almost twenty years been a friend, guide, and inspiration. His example in his pastoral care and his homilies has been a major factor in my taking the risk to nakedly present my thoughts on faith and church. Frank Dumont, PhD, retired professor of psychology at McGill University, has been an intellectual gadfly and personal friend over a forty-five-year period. Our discussions in person, through the mail or on e-mail have been both a joy and a spur. His challenges to me have helped me sharpen my thoughts and even recognize some flaws. Dr. Cris Villapando, along with his wife Guia, has helped me through some difficult times, and they have been a source of encouragement in my faith exploration and expression.

I want to mention a small group of fellow parishioners from Father Carl's Sacred Heart Parish. We have been meeting biweekly for over three years, and the group is made up of five couples and a widower. We call ourselves the Faith Group, and we evolved from a parish-wide look at an adult faith formation program called Why Catholic? After a few sessions, we decided that the canned program did not fit our needs, and we began an open-discussion group where we use writings by authors such as Richard Rohr, OFM, and Anthony de Mello, SJ, as stimulus or provocative agent. I value the other ten members as close friends, as persons with whom I can share openly and know I will be received with care and compassion, and also as a group where humor and laughter resound on Thursday evenings. To each of those persons, I want to say this: You people are, in a real sense, the cause of this volume. Without you, it would probably never have been written. So thank you to Susan Petersen, my wife; Pat Bohan; Larry and JoAnne Doyle; David and Jan Ledwig; Tom and Bonnie McMahon; and Ray and Barb Norris.

For six years, I have been privileged to be part of another group that meets weekly. We have no name. We spend Tuesday mornings exploring spiritual matters and exploring our own ideas and feelings. This is a very religiously heterogeneous group where as agnostics, Buddhists, Catholics, Episcopalians, or Unitarian Universalists, we discover that both love and wisdom spring forth from all backgrounds. It is our humanness that ties us together. I thank them for giving me comfort, insight, and challenge even if I am usually the only male present at our sessions.

To all mentioned above, living and deceased, my heartfelt thanks. You have all been occasions of grace for me and still are.

—

INTRODUCTION

I HAVE HAD A lifelong love affair with the Catholic Church though that affair has travelled some bumpy roads. I suppose that this document could be described as falling someplace between a love letter and a plea for a hearing. I know that it will seem to some readers that I have more than my share of chutzpah even to consider writing these pages. I make no claim of expertise or unusual knowledge in theology or scripture or church history. I am what might be described as a dabbler in those fields. So what do I bring to this task, and why should anyone care about this layman's perspective?

I love my church even as I feel burdened and disappointed by the actions of Church leaders, both here in the United States and throughout the world. I have been a Catholic almost as long as Pope Benedict XVI, and I identify myself with this church. I was brought up in a traditional Catholic family, but not one given to displays of piety. In my early years, we lived in communities where being Catholic made us somewhat marginal, but my parents remained proud of their faith and practiced it with what I now would call gentle defiance. I have faced some minor discrimination because of my religious affiliation, but these have been more than balanced by advantages, which have come to me because of my Catholic belief and heritage.

So why am I writing this book? I have taken my cue from the fathers of the Church in their expressed need to "read the signs of the times" as the Second Vatican Council worked to bring the Church's style and mode of interaction with the world up-to-date. Pope John XXIII, in his remarks at the opening session of the council, emphasized that the work of the council was to have a focus on the pastoral role of the Church, and he underlined his preference for the "medicine of mercy" rather than of severity. I hope that these pages, in some small way, will reflect Blessed John XXIII's aspirations.

I fear that tradition and habit have sometimes replaced serious consideration of the implications of the council's teaching on the primacy of the individual conscience and the corollary requirement of forming a "right" conscience. In fact, the council's focus on the dignity of the human person often seems pushed to the background. I do not accept the idea that studying, discerning, and praying to bring about a "well-formed conscience" (*Catechism of the Catholic Church*, para. 1783) will automatically result in 100 percent conformity with the teachings of the magisterium. Indeed, human behavior is often confronted with complex situations that call for prudential judgments in the face of competing values. The Gospel stories frequently record Jesus's emphasis on the need to interpret the law in a context of priorities. I sense a rigidity and an unwholesome desire to have the past replace the present among some of our clergy and hierarchy; those tendencies seem to me to be rooted in fear and in lack of trust in the Holy Spirit's presence throughout the universe.

That reactionary trend seems counter to the council's call for openness and dialogue. My hope here is to express my concern for the Church's future especially in the role of calling all people to "holiness" and toward helping to bring about the kingdom. While I take as foundational John's Gospel and letters with the emphasis on God as love, I also wish to underline the role that human emotions, needs, and values play in our faith and spiritual life. As I make this effort, I wish to do so with respect for those who may disagree with me. My defense against those who may doubt my sincerity or intentions is simply to say that I love the Catholic Church, but I also know that the whole of the law, as Jesus taught, can be reduced to those two commandments: love of God and love of neighbor. My goal is that the pages that follow will reflect my effort to embrace those commandments.

Let me add just a few autobiographical notes, which will neither explain nor excuse (whichever may be desired) my writing. They may, however, allow the reader to understand where my perceptions, values, and concerns come from.

I spent seven years as a seminarian preparing for ordination to the diocesan priesthood. In that process, I earned both a bachelor's degree and a master's degree in philosophy. I left the seminary as my theological studies were in their early stage. I have served as a psychological consultant to two bishops with most of my work having to do with the psychological evaluation of persons seeking to be accepted as seminarians for a diocese or religious order with an occasional professional relationship with priests experiencing doubts or problems. I helped design and bring into being an experimental Catholic elementary school in an African American section of the city; this school became a magnet for both African American and Caucasian students. I served as the diocesan director of faith formation and superintendent of Catholic schools where I had twenty-three elementary schools and three high schools with a student population of over seven thousand under my purview; later, I became the director of Synod Implementation and Diocesan Planning for the same diocese. During those years, I was also a member of the Diocesan Curia. After retiring from those roles, I designed and played a leadership role in a vicariate faith formation leadership team that brought together ten parishes for planning and sharing resources. In my own parish, I have been the director of faith formation and have chaired our pastoral council. I was proud and honored that Pope John Paul II named me a knight commander in the Order of St. Gregory the Great in 1997, and I felt similarly honored when the Theological College at the Catholic University of America selected me to be the second recipient of the Joseph Cardinal Bernardin Medal.

READING THE SIGNS OF THE TIMES

AS I MENTIONED in the introduction, being a Catholic has been a source of joy and comfort to me. That is not to say that I have always been happy with the Church, with its leaders or with its "teachings." In fact, I have found myself, on occasion, in conflict, if not with the teaching itself and with the hierarchy's interpretation of the teaching. I would expect that the Church—which, at least, since Vatican II, has given primacy to the dignity of the person and to the individual conscience—would expect honest disagreement and strong dialogue over issues that pertain to human behavior. So I find myself in this second decade of the twenty-first century wondering why this church, which I love and respect, finds itself accused of irrelevance by many. What causes the fog that obscures, to the eyes of many, the beauty, love, and compassion that keeps me faithful?

While the increasingly secular culture where greed continues to be seen as some sort of virtue and where deceit along with arrogance is accepted as a road to support that virtue, there are also events over the last few decades that have dulled the prophetic voice of the Church. In the American Church, which so clearly made sexual transgression the cornerstone of sin for over two centuries, often ignoring the far more corrosive influence of greed on families and society as a whole, the pedophile scandal has eaten away trust and credibility. Some of those men of the cloth who decried the evil of premarital or extramarital sex were themselves sexually molesting children and adolescents. I suspect that it has done even more fundamental damage. In my career, I have known and worked with over one hundred priests. Many have been outstanding examples—holy, learned, and compassionate. Even more have been honestly striving to become that example with mixed success; a few have been joyless, rigid, and closed minded. As an aside, in the closing decades of the twentieth century when I was involved in the psychological evaluations of applicants to the seminary, I had the clear impression that this last category had become increasingly present. Despite the very small percentage of priests who have precipitated this scandal, the priesthood as a sacred commitment is called into question.

Equally troubling has been the collusion of the hierarchy in ignoring and, in some cases, deliberately hiding these priestly transgressions. We are speaking here about serious crimes, more heinous than forcible rape of an adult, and the perception of many (including myself) is that some Church leaders have been more concerned about protecting the Church image and avoiding or reducing civil liability actions than in providing pastoral care. The pedophile scandal, while the most troublesome of the events bringing Church policy and actions to public notice, is not the only problem area. For me, it is difficult to understand the actions of some bishops and archbishops who have been denying the Eucharist to lawmakers who fail to support the call for legislation prohibiting abortion. To my knowledge, most of these legislators have publicly stated their personal opposition to abortion, but they are reluctant to impose their view on a pluralistic constituency. That seems to me as a matter of conscience: they accept the magisterium's teaching that abortion is intrinsically evil, but their conscience holds them back from supporting action to create legal sanctions. That sounds like a position clearly allowable under the *Catechism of the Catholic Church* (para. 1782) which states, quoting in part the Vatican II *Declaration on Religious Liberty:* "Man has the right to act in conscience and in freedom so as personally to make moral decisions. 'He must not be forced to act contrary to his conscience. Nor must he be prevented from acting according to his conscience." The argument, of course, will be that those lawmakers have not developed a right conscience, but does that mean that any variation from the teaching of a local bishop is, de facto, evidence of failure "to discern the will of God expressed in divine law"?

Since I have just mentioned ecclesiastical restrictions on the reception of the Eucharist, I want to share another policy which clouds the brightness of the loving, compassionate Church, which I really believe has the commission to be Jesus's presence in the world. Remember, Jesus fed the crowds with the loaves and fish. There were great numbers of followers, but there were no restrictions on who was to be fed. No one asked if a person was in a gay or lesbian relationship or in an adulterous one. Jesus's desire was to feed the hungry. Somehow I see the Eucharist as a continuation of that invitation. After all, Jesus told us that he came to save the sinner, and he assured us that those who eat his body will have life everlasting.

Why are the divorced who have remarried barred from this food? Yes, Jesus did clearly state that divorce was not condoned, but he did not withhold his blessing from the Samaritan woman at the well who had enjoyed many husbands. Can it be that Jesus, in his comment about divorce, was expressing an ideal that all married couples should strive to meet rather than indicate a category of persons to be excluded from his gift of love? Since diocesan marriage tribunals can declare a marriage invalid because of psychological immaturity, would it be far-fetched to presume that in a majority of cases where the marriage has failed, one or both of the parties was psychologically unprepared for the commitment? To me, that presumption sounds more Christian than denying to persons the "source and summit" of our spiritual life.

In the area of medical ethics, the Church commits itself to being the advocate for life for those who are least able to speak for themselves. Yet to many (including me), that voice is a voice of harshness and lack of compassion. In the realm of those whose lives have been reduced to a vegetative state, what constitutes extraordinary interventions? Intravenous feeding for months and years when there are no signs of conscious awareness or brain activity certainly seems to me to be pretty extraordinary. How do we square the emphasis on life and even more the importance of compassion for the living when the overwhelming medical opinion that mother and fetus will both die unless the fetus is terminated? When a dedicated nun wrestles with this issue and finally decides that the removal of the fetus is the only way to preserve the life of the mother/wife, her decision (after the fact) is second-guessed by diocesan authorities, and the nun is excommunicated by the local bishop for aiding in a direct abortion. I cannot picture Jesus, facing the husband and the woman, coldly condemning her to death knowing that the unborn child will die with her. (I am aware that some medical persons argue that there were medical reasons that would result in the action being an indirect abortion, but even in the form of a direct abortion, I would argue that Church teaching, on following one's conscience, would trump the written law—prudential judgment has to have primacy.)

Then, of course, in the realm of sexual issues, there are three areas where many of the faithful feel that the Church's teaching is inconsistent with Christ's message of love. First, the continuing ban on artificial methods of preventing conception is, if we can believe the many polls on that issue, ignored by the majority of Catholics of childbearing age. This is ironic in that the *Catechism of the Catholic Church* (para. 1601) along with *The Code of Canon Law, 1983 Revision* (para. 1055) both place the purpose of marriage "for the good of the spouses" before the "procreation and education of offspring." Earlier official Church documents had indicated that "procreation and education" were the primary purpose of marriage. That change combined with the Church's stance on intent as a major factor in culpability makes me wonder why natural family planning receives Church blessing while the use of the pill does not. The intent in both instances is to avoid pregnancy; the only difference is that the risk of having the method fail is greater in natural family planning. The pill controls ovulation while the thermometer tries to predict ovulation, yet both have the same goal: reducing the risk of conception.

A second area of controversy relates to premarital sex and cohabitation. The old norm of delaying intercourse (especially for women!) until after the marriage ceremony has, in many quarters, gone by the wayside. I have no data on the percentage of couples who have, so to speak, consummated the marriage before speaking their vows in a ceremony, either civil or religious, but I feel certain that it would be a significant percentage. I have heard that issue summarized by "what difference does a piece of paper make?"

Then there is the growing acceptance of same-sex marriages in the general public. This third issue seems to be particularly troublesome to the hierarchy as well as many religiously conservative persons/groups. Despite this opposition, tolerance of accepting these unions of love and care as marriages is on the upswing. What bothers many, including this author, about the resistance of Church representatives to this movement is not their disagreement over the use of the term "marriage"; it is their resort to fear tactics by predicting terrible things will happen to the institution of marriage and harm will come to children living in such homes when the bishops must know that the little evidence available contradicts those assertions. In any event, I find it difficult to picture Jesus condemning a relationship of love, care, fidelity, and joy. In fact, such a relationship seems to describe the "good" marriage.

This litany of problem areas where the Church's behavior and/or image is tarnished in the eyes of many (sometimes with good reason, sometimes unfairly) cannot exclude the limitations on the official role of women in the Church. The prohibition of ordination of women to either the permanent diaconate or the priesthood is a stumbling block for many. The traditional argument that Jesus was male and so the priest, sometimes described as an *alter Christus* (another Christ), must also be male finds little resonance with many, especially in the light of Jesus's relationship with women (somewhat startling in the culture in which he lived), in the elevation of female saints to the title of doctors of the Church, and in the increasing number of female theologians teaching priests-to-be in seminaries. Not to mention that it was a woman whose words ("let it be done to me according to your words") first brought the body and blood of Jesus into this world. Could one argue that since that event depended on a woman, should women be especially appropriate to call on the Holy Spirit to transform the bread and wine into the body and blood of Jesus?

I am not suggesting that the Church should embrace positions simply because they are popular or are becoming popular; I am praying that the Church will be sensitive to the psychological and spiritual (yes, spiritual!) dynamics that lie behind these phenomena. For me, that means more than condemning the evils of the world and hiding behind the mantra "error has no rights." Blessed Pope John XXIII, in his opening remarks at the council, expressly disagreed with the prophets of doom who see nothing but catastrophe in the trends of the modern world. One of the landmark accomplishments of the council is the Pastoral Constitution on the Church in the Modern World *(Gaudium et Spes)* where the Church commits itself to honest interaction with the world and to dialogue with all in the pursuit of what Jesus, in the Gospels, calls the kingdom.

One of the serious problems confronting the Church is the lack of a vibrant faith among many of the baptized. My observation is that this malaise cuts across age groups, ethnic backgrounds, and gender. Even those who, when asked, will identify themselves as Catholic and even are reasonably well-versed in Catholic teaching are often only nominal Catholics (or Christians). For example, the concept of sin has become trivialized mostly in my eyes because it has been poorly conceptualized and even more poorly taught. The current controversy over the wording in the Liturgy of the Mass in its English form is symptomatic of behaviors that suggest "fiddling while Rome—the Vatican—burns." Where do we hear the emphasis on the Mass as a dialogue of love between God and the "people of God," a dialogue that ends with a call to go forth and transform the world? Instead, we have great energy and time spent in substituting consubstantial for "one in body" and "enter under my roof" for "receive you." The resources that will go into the promulgation and adoption of those verbal modifications will necessarily detract from the resources available to proclaim the Gospel and work to bring about the kingdom. I seriously doubt that these changes to make the English Mass almost a literal translation of the Latin (even where at times the Latin is farther from the even earlier Greek than the current English!) will do much toward filling the hearts of the faithful or inflaming in those hearts the fire of divine love.

It is easy to diagnose problems and weaknesses; the challenge is to wrestle with designs and actions that may alleviate those situations. Still, it is first necessary to acknowledge the ailment and to accept responsibility for our participation in its cause and its continuance. Scapegoats are useless;

blaming others is equally nonproductive. The question for each of us is, what can I do? Behind that question is the presumption that I (each of us) want the problem to be healed. The Western world (the same may be true for the East as well, but I will restrict my comment to an area where I feel confident of the relevance of my remarks) is infected with a culture of fear. Blessed Pope John Paul II preferred to describe a similar pattern of symptoms as a "culture of death," but the evidence in my mind points to fear with its companions of paranoia, self-righteousness, and deception as the main issue. We, in the Church, have contributed to this pervasive infection that destroys trust and poisons the thrust toward community. Ironically, the lack of trust has now clouded the image of the Church. Yet we know the antidote to fear; it is given to us in 1 John where he writes, "There is no fear in love, but perfect love drives out fear" (4:18).

In the pages that follow, I wish to share some thoughts on how Catholic spiritual development (I like that term better than "faith formation") might take a more radical and less dogmatic approach as it assists the faithful, along with some new explorers of the faith, in pursuing holiness as well as working to bring about the kingdom. These thoughts and views will have their roots in the Christian scriptures, in the writings of Thomas Aquinas, and in my personal experience. I hope that they will evoke discussion and perhaps even open new vistas for some readers. At the heart of my undertaking this journey is my embrace of Vatican II's frequent mention of the dignity of the human person and the simple words of Georges Bernanos's priest protagonist in the novel *Diary of a Country Priest* who stated as he was dying, *"Grace is everywhere."*

WHY DOES GOD EXIST?

WHY DOES GOD exist may sound like an audacious question or perhaps like a stupid one. Yet to me, it is a fundamental question. *The Catechism of the Catholic Church* (para. 31-35) describes "ways of coming to know God," which includes the study and awareness of the order and beauty of the universe and goes beyond St. Anselm of Canterbury's oft-cited "ontological argument" for God's existence. As a child, I went through all the questions and answers of the *Baltimore Catechism,* but it was simply an exercise in memory. My learning did not really mean much to me. I was in the ninth grade before I felt a need for God, and suddenly, I knew that God existed. It is the experience of God that seems in my mind the profound basis for asserting God's existence. As we look at the many eons of human history and even at the evidence of our human prehistory, it appears that some perception of god—of a being or beings more powerful than we humans, a being upon whom we are in various ways dependent—is present in all cultures. I would suggest that this phenomenon is tied to intrinsic human needs, especially the needs for answers, for belongingness, and for forgiveness. In a sense, I would say that God exists because we need God.

St. Augustine of Hippo captured what I believe is the essence of this innate longing or need with his comment that the "heart is restless until it rests in Thee." Those words underline the quest for belonging, for relationship. The long history of sacrifice to the various gods (which in many cultures included human sacrifice) attests to a need for appeasing the gods and seeking forgiveness for transgressions. And even today we find persons who attribute to some divine being the cause of natural and even human-caused catastrophe, which are seen as punishment for sins.

That short paragraph points up the dual nature of the human perception of the divinity across time and culture. Even in the Hebrew scriptures, there is a theme of a vengeful god who punishes his chosen people for disobedience. The Christian message, as I hear it, is at odds with that tradition. The Christ-based tradition defines God as love (1 John 4:18), and if we accept the message in Genesis that we humans are created "in the image of God," then *love* must be central to our being also. For me, it is a simple and natural step from there to see that Augustine's "restless heart" is the innate call for each of us to reach out to that *love* that is the source of our being.

In fact, our human lives are built around relationships, and in our sometimes-weird ways, we spend much of our lives pursuing relationships that will give us belongingness, acceptance, and purpose. How often do we hear of someone in her or his closing days commenting on how only the relationships, still active or even lost, have lasting value? Of course, relationships can also be a source of deep pain and the occasion for a profound sense of loss. I can still recall the feeling of bewilderment when, after seven years of preparing for the Catholic priesthood, I left the seminary. In actual fact, over those years, all my deep friendships had been with fellow seminarians, and I looked to the continuation of many of those friendships. Unfortunately, that was not to be. It was as if I had disappeared off the face of the earth. Not one answered my letters, and in fact, I heard from only one of my many colleagues, and that was after his ordination, some four years later.

My deciding to leave the seminary came about because I felt an incompleteness, a restless heart, a longing for a more intimate physical relationship. I had struggled for months with the hope that my emotional and cognitive relationship with Jesus would fulfill that need. Sad to say, my spiritual maturity had not developed to that level at the age of twenty-two. I would learn that the restlessness of my heart would surface again and again until I came to believe in and trust Jesus as the God of wild love and reckless giving. I have never had a vision nor has Jesus spoken to me. I am delighted with the sense of his presence when I attend to him—and sometimes when I least expect it. The image of Francis Thompson's poem, "The Hound of Heaven," is my frequent companion. I picture Jesus as a persistent and gentle basset hound, following me down "the labyrinthine ways of my own mind" and sniffing me out from behind my fig leaf and several masks. He seeks the real, the naked me whom he loves, not the one I have pretended to be. I cannot prove that these feelings are truly Jesus's presence; nonetheless, I rejoice in them, and it is this personal relationship with Jesus that ties me to the Church.

The point of this short autobiographical comment is to illustrate what seems to have been lost in the Church's interaction with the world today. Ours is a world that is hurting. The culture of fear, which permeates our world, finds the very central themes of Jesus's message difficult to embrace. Community and unity are at the heart of the Gospel message. But in this world, diversity often shades into divisiveness. Differences of opinion or interpretation give rise to anger. Suspicion of others creates paranoia, anger, and enmity. Jesus's condensing of the commandments down to the two that encompass the whole moral code—love God and love your neighbor—seems out of place in this fearful world. Where is the Christian church? We claim to be a counterculture, but our words and actions often suggest that we are accomplices in this dehumanizing culture of fear. I am reminded of a quip of G. K. Chesterton about Christianity: "*The Christian ideal has not been tried and found wanting. It has been found difficult . . . and left untried.*" Thomas Wolfe, the prolific writer and author of the novels *Look Homeward, Angel* and *You Can't Go Home Again,* in his piece "The Anatomy of Loneliness" describes the stumbling block with Christ's message in more personal terms. The following excerpt captures his thought.

> *The gospels of the New Testament . . . become the chronicle of the life of love. What Christ is always saying, what he never swerves from saying, what he says a thousand times in a thousand different ways, but always with a central unity of belief, is this: "I am my Father's son, and you are my brothers." And the unity that binds us all together, that makes this earth a family, and all men brothers and sons of God, is love.*

> *The central purpose of Christ's life, therefore, is to destroy the life of loneliness and to establish here on earth the life of love . . . And I know that though the way and meaning of Christ's life is a far, far better way and meaning than my own, yet I can never make it mine.*

To paraphrase these thoughts, where and how do we find the courage to bring together communities through love, to conquer that sense of loneliness or isolation suggested in Augustine's writing about the restless heart? How do we escape from the prison of fear where we come together in a spirit of vigilance and hostile expectation, where that fear poisons our perceptions and creates barriers among peoples?

With Wolfe, as I have stated above, I feel deeply that the only antidote to fear is love. Yet as Jesus's life clearly illustrates, love flourishes in a context of vulnerability, openness, and integrity. Those three words are clearly not frequent descriptors of the media's portrayal of the Church's behavior in the recent scandals, and certainly, the Roman Curia has earned its reputation for secrecy and clandestine workings. The question, "If salt shall lose its savor, with what shall it be salted?" comes easily to mind. Thomas Aquinas reminds us that *"no person can live without delight and that is why those deprived of spiritual joy seek carnal pleasures."*

If we combine John's definition of God as love, Augustine's claim of the restless heart, and Thomas Aquinas's bald statement that the quest of delight (pleasure?) is a central component of human life, what would a church look like built on that foundation? How would those simple statements about the nature of God and the nature of the human person shape our interpretation of the incarnation, life, and resurrection of Jesus? What would be the implications for the content of a catechism that retained the fourfold structure of the *Catechism of the Catholic Church (CCC)*—the profession of faith, the celebration of the Christian mystery, life in Christ, Christian prayer—sometimes simplified to faith professed, faith expressed, faith lived, and faith prayed but had, as its foundational theme, God's unconditional love and the awareness that grace is everywhere? I have neither the knowledge nor the wisdom even to begin such an undertaking, but I do hope to explore some current issues facing my church in the early decades of the twenty-first century.

In the sections to follow, I try to present this layman's perception of such a church with the hope that it may provide some suggestions on how this countercultural church, reflecting the love of the Creator, Teacher, and Sanctifier, might stir the hearts of many, encourage holiness, and gather together the people of God in assisting to bring about the kingdom of God.

This is in no way to suggest that the pages that follow are in any fashion designed to supplement or to modify the *Catechism.* That volume is a rich resource and reference tool, helpful to those teaching what has been and what is. It is a compendium of the Church's teaching and a valuable reference for anyone seeking deeper knowledge of the Catholic faith. My interest is in what could be if we simply applied some basic but central teachings of Jesus to the life situations confronting the people of God today. In the paragraph above, I mentioned the rephrasing of the *Catechism's* four parts into action statements: faith *professed, expressed, lived,* and *prayed.* My hope is to interface those actions with the culture of the twenty-first century in the United States and explore some suggestions about how the treasure of the Catholic faith might become more open and vibrant in that context.

FAITH: HOW, WHAT, WHY?

HOW DO WE come to a belief in a god, especially a god who is all-powerful and all-knowing, but even a god who is creator of the universe? The *CCC* speaks of the possibility of discerning this latter god from our observations of nature with its order and beauty. We know that many pagan religions were organized around powerful, anthropomorphic gods. The Hebrew scriptures present us with a God above all gods who governs the universe and holds his people with whom he has made a covenant to standards of behavior and worship. But faith, at its roots, is a human assent, a choice, which flows from many sources. For the Christian, faith is a gift, but in some mysterious ways, it is a gift open to all—even those who have never heard of Jesus. To those of us who have the experience of learning about Jesus, this gift comes handed down through the centuries and carries with it a way of life. The passage from Thomas Wolfe quoted earlier is an example of the challenge of that faith. To Wolfe, the message is clear and beautiful, but the expectations are beyond his willingness to accept.

It seems that there are at least three issues implicit in the concept of faith: the content or the "what" of faith, how we respond to that content, and what the implications of faith for my life are (or are there any?). The initial section of the *CCC* deals with the content of what we believe while the other three sections provide guidelines for our responding and living in the world. Debates have raged around the content of Christian belief since shortly after the death of Jesus. The several councils of the early Church were mostly called to settle differences in belief and practice. The multiplication of communities with varying histories and values perceived developed different facets or interpretations as central and critical to the essence of the faith. These facts attest to the continuous diversity of perception of the Gospel message(s). But more pressing for the individual believer is how to respond to that message. Am I skeptical of it? Do I see the message as an ideal? Do I feel called to a commitment? Let me suggest that our level of belief varies from item to item, but through them, the basic question revolves around trust. For example, I heartily believe in all the statements of the Nicene Creed; on the other hand, I also accept such derived teachings as the bodily assumption of Mary, the mother of Jesus, into heaven as a wonderful idea. If suddenly, her bodily remains were discovered in a dig in the area around Ephesus, my basic faith would not be shaken. I would simply drop that as a dogma of my faith.

In a Kierkegaardian framework, we are asking, Do I have the courage to leap? Am I aware of the risks? Can I make the choice? Kierkegaard sees faith as the passionate clinging to something uncertain. St. Paul writes that faith is "the assurance of things hoped for." So it seems that faith is built on trust and looks to the future. It is a very personal experience though it often takes place in a community with community support. The catalog of beliefs fills out that faith and provides some cognitive foundation, but I would suggest that faith itself is an act of choice that reflects our emotional and value characteristics. In organized faith systems, core beliefs become expanded by what I see as peripheral items, which enrich (but may also complicate) our assent. For example, I recognize the interior struggle that we humans have between our ego and our longing for a personal relationship with God. I believe that the allegory of Adam and Eve in the Garden of Eden tells the story of that struggle. However, since I do not believe that Adam and Eve were the first humans from whom all of us are descended, the concept of original sin makes no sense. What St. Augustine described with that term is the struggle that I mentioned above. Why do we need to accept the Adam and Eve story as historical fact to explain our human tendency toward putting self first when no such story exists to explain the existence of fallen angels? (See *Catechism*, para. 391-395.) And if I reject the original sin idea, then the doctrine of the Immaculate Conception of Mary makes no sense. But I honor Mary and her holiness, and I feel that her role as the mother of Jesus makes her, in a sense, the first priest bringing Jesus to the world. So even though I cannot embrace the idea of the Immaculate Conception, I am willing to use that title as symbolic of her holiness and special importance.

Faith is a personal choice, and as I would use the term, it is the affirmation of a relationship with God. It goes beyond reason and gathers its vitality in the experiential and affective domains. It comes from a deep yearning or longing (to again use a Kierkegaard term) and provides both substance and direction to life. In many ways, this personal faith is a confrontive response to the secular society, the culture of fear that has infected the Western world since the days of the Enlightenment; our faith is a cry that the material world minus its spiritual soul is lifeless. The adherents to the belief that there is no meaning to life beyond this sensate world may have found a road to make life easy since there are no worries about a life after death, but that easiness is sadly empty. Faith moves us beyond the realm of scientific objectivity (though there are scientists who see the quantum mechanics views as opening doors to the intersection of the spiritual with the material) and leads us to wrestle with the meaning of life and its purpose: not only why do I exist, but also what am I to do?

If God is love and faith is our self-chosen response to that love, what can we say about that god? First and foremost, God is a personal god; God is not just a force nor is s/he the universe. Jesus regularly calls God as father, and he, time and again, speaks of the Father's awareness of and the ability to intervene in the events of the planet earth. The great strength of the Christ-based religion is the conviction that Jesus is God made flesh and the record of his life on this earth as portrayed in the four Gospels clearly illustrates a message of love. While the four evangelists vary considerably in presenting facets of Jesus, they agree on his emphases on forgiveness, acceptance, compassion, and love. They also, in differing ways, underline some basic themes in Jesus's teaching, including community, conversion, the cross, and nonviolence.

That inadequate synopsis of the Christ-message already makes clear that the message of Jesus—and, therefore, the message that the Church must reflect to be true to its founder—is a challenge to the world of the twenty-first century. The variation of content and emphasis on aspects of Jesus's teaching among the evangelists probably is related both to the personality of the writer and the writer's intent. Still, those four themes mentioned in the previous paragraph seem represented in all four Gospels. So in the coming pages, we will ask ourselves how they fit in today's world. Better yet, perhaps we should ask, what does the disconnection between the world of the twenty-first century and the Christ-message mean to me personally? Those questions bring us face-to-face with my faith, with what I really believe deep down.

A beginning answer goes as follows: I believe in a personal God who has created the universe out of love, who in the person of Jesus took on our humanity in order to show us how to live with love, who continues to be present throughout creation as a source of love available to all. This belief has no dependence upon ontological or "first mover" *proofs* of God's existence nor on human sciences. I believe because I find myself searching for this God and aspiring to be her/his follower because those aspirations call me to be a better person than I might otherwise try to be. I cannot prove to anybody the truth of that belief; I can only share it. Do I have any doubt about that belief? I recognize that I might be in error because my world typically looks for objective or scientific evidence to support such claims, but I feel confident that this God of wild love and reckless giving exists, permeates the world with goodness, and calls all humans to live the way of love. I live on confidence rather than on certainty.

Central to that perception of God is the gift to us of free will, the gift of having the opportunity to shape our own lives through our choices. The challenge of creating our own lives certainly differs depending upon many circumstances, especially the differing settings that our ancestors have developed since human beings walked upright on this planet. In other words, we do not all start from the same life conditions—either in assets/gifts or in challenges/burdens. The era in which we are born, the country and environment where we are born, and the family to which we are born are all factors beyond our choice or control as are such crises as living in the midst of widespread hunger or war or natural calamities like earthquakes, tsunamis, or hurricanes. Despite this unevenness in life conditions, we are all responsible for how we respond, whether as a direct participant or as an observer. Will our responses flow from our commitment to love, or will they reflect on how fear holds us captive?

People raise a legitimate and troubling question: how does a God of love allow these striking differences and these cruel events? I cannot answer that question. Does it bother me? Of course, it bothers me, but at the same time, those inexplicable conditions and/or events are at the heart of faith. Faith is not, in my mind, a security blanket to make life easier and less troublesome. Faith is a call, and in my faith, that call is for me and my fellow believers to create a new way of interacting in the world, the way that Jesus taught us even at the cost of his human life. That way is the way of unconditional love, a very demanding standard that I (and I suspect most human beings) frequently find extremely difficult to maintain. Jesus's life makes clear that this way is not easy and often is scorned and rejected. Is it not reasonable that a similar fate will often be our experience? So for me, the issue is not why is there all of this unfairness, cruelty, and catastrophe. The question is, what will I do about it? How can I, in my little world, work to create the climate of love—the climate of forgiveness, of acceptance, of compassion, and of unconditioned sharing?

Faith is the force behind how I choose to live. It is, as I have said, rooted in trust, inspired by the Jesus of the Gospels, and nourished by the remarkable survival of the Church despite the episodes of un-Christlike behaviors such as the Crusades, the Inquisition, the embrace of cruel political regimes, the demeaning of the dignity of the person of the nonbeliever, and the immoral

THOMAS W. MAHAN

arrogance of some of its leaders. Jesus told us that he came to save the sinner, so is it not appropriate that his human church should need saving as well? In fact, it seems that Jesus was more disturbed by institutional or organizational sin than by individual shortcomings. We have clear evidence that the Holy Spirit does not protect the hierarchy from making stupid or foolish decisions or judgments nor has the Spirit kept me from doing the same. It would be nice to think that the Holy Spirit would keep Church authorities from setting forth policies or making general pronouncements that are in error. Unfortunately, such a belief is contradicted time and again by painful facts; indeed, the idea that the bishop is the authentic and authoritative interpreter of Church teaching within his diocese strikes me as overreaching, especially in these days when we face many complex actual and potential situations. Like Solomon, bishops should ask for an understanding heart (note the term "heart" rather than "mind"—could that imply the need for compassion?) while seeking counsel from specialists as well as the persons affected by decisions.

Another way of phrasing my concerns interacting with my faith is to underline my belief in Jesus as "God with us," as the human incarnation of the God of wild love and reckless giving, but to recognize how imperfectly his apostles understood his teaching. I find it difficult to believe that the descendants of those apostles are any more protected from error or foolishness than the originals. Much as I treasure the coming of the Holy Spirit at Pentecost and believe that the Holy Spirit guides the Church over time, I doubt that such guidance guarantees any human being (or for that matter, groups of human beings or even presumptuous authors!) freedom from error, misjudgment, misperception, or plain stupidity. Each of us, laypersons and clerics, must struggle for ourselves with the help of the community to find truth and to exercise wisdom. The Church has a treasury of teachings and insights to guide us in that struggle, but not to rescue us from wrestling with the issues and probable outcomes as we live and make choices.

Let me suggest that the crowning glory of each of us as created in the image of God is our freedom and ability to make choices. That also is our profound responsibility, which carries with it the risk of falling short, of failing to do the right thing, of hiding the truth, or of hiding under deception. The myth of Adam and Eve tells us the story of God's gift of free will and the unending confrontation we face as we make choices. (I use the word myth to describe a "traditional story to explain some practice, rite or phenomenon of nature.") I eagerly applaud the Church's teaching that all life is precious and that the taking of a life on the face of it is always wrong. Then we come face-to-face with hard choices. Is there an exception to save my own life? Is there an exception in war? Is there an exception for capital punishment for serious crimes? Is there an exception to save the life of a pregnant mother?

Bishops generally seem to leave to civil authorities the decision on the rightness of taking a life in all those cases except the last (which seems, to a husband and father, the most obvious case for allowing the destruction of a life). Why? How is the unborn child more precious than the innocent collateral damage in modern warfare (which often probably includes the killing of the unborn as well as the fully living!)? I had a professor in my graduate studies, the Reverend Charles Hart, PhD, who would remind us regularly that "life laughs at logic." General principles are great as guidelines for our decisions, but they cannot, in my view, replace the well-formed conscience in the crucible of concrete experience.

Some of my statements in the preceding pages may be misunderstood. Let me try to clarify my position on three issues. The first has to do with the clergy, essentially bishops and priests. I have deep respect for Catholic priests and bishops. I admire their courage, their commitment, and their lives of service. I look to them as spiritual guides and agents of forgiveness, acceptance, and compassion—in that sense, as an alter Christus (another Christ). I accept their special role whereby they are not only the fleshly representative of God's forgiveness, but also the ones who can call down his Holy Spirit to bring us the Eucharist. Joseph Cardinal Bernardin, then archbishop of Chicago, wrote, "The priest is called to be challenger, enabler, life-giver, poet of life, music-maker, dreamer of dreams." I have known those priests. They are an inspiration, they call forth awareness of Jesus's presence, and they more than erase for me the pedophile scandal. At the same time, I recognize that ordination does not protect these men from the passions, the temptations, and the weaknesses that are part of being human. To me, that means that their judgments and decisions are fallible. Indeed, the early Church wrestled with the efficacy of the ordained priest in his role as minister of the sacraments, including the Mass, if he should himself have committed a serious sin without seeking forgiveness or even no longer believe.

The official decision was to say that, in the hands of a duly authorized minister, efficacy came from carrying out the rite, not from the spiritual status of the minister. (The Latin term adopted was "ex opere operato," not "ex opere operantis.") So if our priests are subject to the same human experiences and limitations as we, the same strengths and deficits of knowledge and reasoning, the same influences from our emotional life and unconscious as the rest of humanity, each believer must test the judgments and decisions of the priest or bishop against her/his knowledge, analysis, and conscience when dealing with concrete life situations. There is no easy way out of personal responsibility for choices. The knowledge base that many of the ordained draw upon may, in fact, cloud their prudential judgment in concrete situations.

Another area where my comments may be misinterpreted has to do with my understanding of Jesus's intent in some of his teachings as recorded by the evangelists. First, I am no scripture scholar. Even so, it seems to me that Jesus sometimes sets forth for us ideals that he knows that we humans will not meet universally. For example, in his dealing with the rich young man wanting to become perfect, he counsels him to sell everything and come follow him. I think that it is obvious that Jesus did not expect everybody to follow that route. He was setting forth an ideal. Certainly, the Christian churches have treated that episode as such. I believe that the same may be the case with his teachings on divorce. But we need to keep in mind the overall foundational teaching on love of God, love of neighbor (and stranger), and love of self.

Marriage in the Western world in the twenty-first century varies greatly from the customs in Palestine in Jesus's time. The role of women in society and before the law is dramatically different. Even the Church teaching on the purpose of marriage has taken a different focus. The reform pope, St. Gregory the Great, writing in the sixth century CE, stated that enjoyment of sexual intimacy was sinful though for married couples it was only a venial sin. For centuries, the Church seemed to accept sexual unions as a necessary evil that was permissible for the procreation of children. Note, however, that both the *1983 Code of Canon Law* (para. 1055) promulgated by Pope John Paul II and the *Catechism of the Catholic Church, Second Edition* (para. 1660) also promulgated by Pope John Paul II in 1997 give primary place "for the good of the spouses" as the purpose of the marriage covenant followed by procreation. In addition, Blessed John Paul II's writings on the theology of the human body attest to a major shift from the days when the body was viewed almost as a sinful burden placing the soul at risk. Thomas Aquinas, seven centuries earlier, wrote, "We ought to cherish the body."

In today's world where the dignity of the human person demands gender equality and shared responsibility, tensions in the relationship may easily develop. These tensions can erode trust between the partners, and love cannot flourish without trust as well as respect. Marriage tribunals in the dioceses often cite psychological immaturity as an impediment to a valid marriage, but I wonder if the death of love between the spouses should not terminate the covenant when that love dies. Marriage as a relationship that is to reflect the union between Christ and the Church cannot exist without love, trust, and respect. Without those three virtues, the marriage dies, and yet scripture tells us that the intent of the Creator is the union of man and woman. It strikes me that divorce, while not the ideal as Jesus clearly states, can be the door to a new life of grace and holiness. The use of the internal forum as a strategy open to pastors to welcome divorced and remarried back to the sacramental life of the Church is a backdoor route, but the time has come for the possibility, without annulment, of the celebration of this new life.

The third possible confusion has to do with my perception of the magisterium, the teaching authority of the Church and how this authority is expressed. The *Catechism of The Catholic Church, Second Edition* (1997) is a rich treasury of the Church's teachings and a wonderful resource with its (English edition) 688 pages of 2,865 items of information. In addition, it contains 216 pages of support information including an index of citations, a general index of topics, an explanation of abbreviations, and a glossary. In other words as indicated earlier, while the *Catechism* does not lend itself to an afternoon read in an easy chair, it is a formidable and a very valuable source of information about the teachings of the Church. I find myself much more appreciative of the Church's expression of its teachings since it has abandoned practices, which I read as demeaning to the dignity of the person such as *The Index of Forbidden Books*, the strict interpretation of the phrase "extra ecclesiam, nulla salus" (outside the Church, there is no salvation), and the terrible assault, including the papal-authorized torture, on human conscience and rights that marked the Church's Inquisition (not to be confused with the Spanish Inquisition, established by the Spanish monarchs in 1479 and still active into the mid-nineteenth century).

Yet even today, in a far more human design, the Church continues to be engaged in ferreting out heretical ideas that might be misleading to the faithful. The writings of theologians who explore new avenues for understanding the dialectic between the divine and the human seem to be especially at risk, and to an outsider, the process intended to allow such writers the opportunity for self-defense appears easily ignored. Even though some of the twentieth century's leading theologians were silenced

THOMAS W. MAHAN

and forbidden to publish their thoughts, yet many later went on to serve at Vatican Council II as periti (experts) to assist the bishops in formulating teachings—some were even named cardinals. This tendency to deny such theologians, usually priests, the freedom to put their ideas into the public forum continues unabated. Among the theologians who faced the humiliation of silencing, but were rehabilitated as experts at Vatican Council II were such influential theologians and innovative thinkers as John Courtney Murray, Pierre Teilhard de Chardin, Henri de Lubac, Yves Congar, and Marie-Dominique Chenu. While Teilhard de Chardin was never brought back to the center stage as an approved author, much less as a council expert, many of his ideas about the omega point and all things converging in Christ found their way into council documents. The innovative thoughts of these men gave the council its vibrancy and appeal to the modern world. Those aberrations of the use of authority that discourage innovation of thought and exploration of ideas appear to me as unfair to the people of God and un-Christlike. Perhaps even worse, such restrictions are counterproductive and demean efforts to bring the Jesus-message to the hungry.

I also recognize that the Church is a human institution proclaiming the Gospel in many very different cultures and through many dramatically changing ages. These cultural changes often impact how we—and the official Church—see situations even though the moral principles may remain stable. We can look at Galileo, who in 1633, after a second appearance before the Inquisition, was ordered not to work to prove Copernicus's revolutionary idea that the sun was the center of our universe and lived under house arrest until his death. In 1979, Pope John Paul II admitted that the Church had erred in its treatment of Galileo. Less dramatic, but still related to questionable public Church positions, are the current teachings (*Catechism*, para. 2414) that clearly prohibit human enslavement of any kind, while even in the time of the War between the States, some bishops of the Catholic Church were staunch defenders of the practice. Then there is the concept of religious freedom as set forth in the declarations of Vatican Council II. The Declaration on Religious Freedom (*Dignitatis Humanae*) flies in the face of earlier Church teaching about the obligation of the state to embrace Catholicism as the true faith. And the teachings on killing human beings are an inconsistent mess.

For a moment, let's look at the issues around the fifth commandment ("thou shall not kill"). The Church is clear and absolute about abortion even to the point where bishops invoke excommunication of persons who, after serious deliberation, allow the killing of the fetus even though that decision is made after medical conclusion that both the mother and the unborn child will die if the fetus is not terminated. (We leave aside whether in the Phoenix, Arizona, case, the action was a direct or indirect abortion, presuming it may have been a direct action against the life of the fetus.) Compare this with the situation of the convicted criminal condemned to death. Has any bishop excommunicated the prosecutor who sought the death penalty or the jurors who voted for it or the governor of the state who failed to commute the sentence? Yet the *Catechism* (para. 2267) quotes Pope John Paul II in his encyclical "Evangelium Vitae" where he writes that the cases where the execution of the offender is an absolute necessity "are very rare if not practically non-existent." To me, this tolerance of state-sanctioned murder seems especially strange when our founder, Jesus Christ, was a victim of such a decree.

Another problem for me is the diversity of the official statements of diocesan bishops who, by canon law, are the authentic teaching voice for their individual dioceses. It is clear that some bishops are at ease in using the Eucharist, the sacrament of love, as a weapon while others apparently feel such decrees are inappropriate. There was a time, in the 1980s, when the bishops of the United States promulgated teachings on social justice for the people of God. Two of these letters seemed to have caused heartburn to some of the US bishops (and probably in Rome). The letters on "The Challenge of Peace" (1983) and "Economic Justice for All" (1986) stand out as examples. However, in 1998, Pope John Paul II distributed an apostolic letter that, for all practical purposes, shut off such pronouncements as authoritative teachings from the various national or area conferences of bishops. John Paul's new guidelines prohibited any such promulgation unless there was *unanimous* agreement of *all* the bishops or, absent such unanimity, a two-thirds vote and the subsequent approval of the Vatican. This suggests to me that the Vatican wants to exercise control and veto over any teachings, which may stir controversy (as "Economic Justice for All" did as it confronted readers with the implications of Catholic teaching on social justice) while still allowing individual bishops to issue decrees that are idiosyncratic and, in the eyes of some, opposed to the spirit of Christ's teaching. The *Code of Canon Law* (1983, para. 753) baldly states, "The faithful must adhere to the authentic teaching of their own bishops with a sense of religious respect." Of course, the bishop himself is the determiner of what is authentic and may even decide what constitutes respect.

THOMAS W. MAHAN

I do not want to close this section on a negative note. I believe that the Catholic Church exists to proclaim the good news of Jesus and that it struggles to explain and describe that good news through human terms. That effort is, of course, doomed to failure; yet even so, the Church remains an imperfect beacon in helping us to know this God whom I describe as the God of wild love and reckless giving and to challenge us to live our lives such that we are part of the effort to bring about the kingdom of forgiveness, acceptance, compassion, and love. Obedience to Church teaching does not mean that we should simply accept the prudential judgments of Church spokesmen. Even though some bishops seem to think otherwise, our consciences—so long as they have seriously considered the concrete situation—must be our final arbiter. Moral judgments and choices are not always easy or straightforward, and no episcopal pronouncement can absolve us from our personal responsibility. We must listen to Church authorities, but each of us is responsible for choosing what we discern is in keeping with Jesus's way of love.

GOD IS LOVE, WE ARE LOVERS

WHAT DOES IT mean to repeat John the Evangelist's words: *God is love*? Paul, in his first letter to the early church at Corinth, describes human love in a beautiful series of adjectives. In that chapter of his letter, Paul used the Greek word "agape," which we translate as love and which St. Jerome, in translating the Greek New Testament into Latin, called amor. The English word "love" (and the Latin "amor") is broader than the Greek "agape"; it includes aspects of what the Greeks called *eros* and *philia*. In fact, as I read it, some of Paul's description of agape (1 Cor. 13) comes close to including elements of both eros and philia. And you may legitimately ask, so what? I see God's love—God as love—as being akin to the passion that we associate with erotic love. Surely the Catholic mystics such as Teresa of Avila use descriptions of their experience of God's presence that call to mind the ecstasy of profound, loving sexual union.

I became enamored of Jesus Christ, God with us in the flesh, when I was in the ninth grade. I was struck by John's simple description of God ("God is love") and Paul's statement that "if I give away everything that I own . . . and do not have love, I gain nothing." Suddenly, faith became alive for me. It was a tremendous gift, and it began a whole new orientation toward life for me. My family situation was burdened by secrets that none of us ever mentioned, and what a relief it was to discover God as a personal relation, as a friend. The abstract God of the *Baltimore Catechism* had become boring and distant. Suddenly, God as Jesus was my companion. I realize that this adolescent discovery is not unusual and is typically short-lived, especially in the light of the growing awareness of more fleshly discoveries. Still, this was a turning point in my life that has continued into my eighth decade of life.

It is interesting for me that love demands both trust and respect. In the world of human relations, those two attributes are necessary if love is more than an emotional high. Many years later, I ran across Thomas Aquinas's comment that "God's love for us is no greater in heaven than it is right here and now." That conviction that God's love is unconditional and unconditioned, that no matter what we do, God's love remains unchanged is a great consolation in difficult times. We can neither earn nor lose God's love. This awareness that love is a gift and that it is up to me to accept it or ignore it or deny it became an insight into how I should model my human loves. That goal made me recognize the wonder of God's gift when I found that it was not easy to put aside hopes or expectations of reciprocity in love. Still, when I was able to do that, my loving became free and freeing. What a joy it is to be a lover, imperfect as I am in that identity.

This is a long way to explaining what being a Catholic Christian means to me. It means making my life goal to be a lover. Of course, the letters of John and James along with the twenty-fifth chapter of Matthew's Gospel spell out that love. If it is more than a dream, it demands action, and for the Christ lover, that means dealing with neighbors and strangers (where Christ is hidden) with forgiveness, acceptance, and compassion. It means sharing my worldly gifts. Where am I to find the courage and strength to express my love to God's creation through this loving and sharing? The gift of grace, which is God's love given to us for the taking, is the answer.

The village priest in Bernanos's novel, *Diary of a Country Priest*, in his dying words states a central Catholic belief when he says to his classmate who has strayed from his priestly vows, *"Grace is everywhere."* When I read the book for the first time as a college freshman, that reality was brought home for me. Grace *is* everywhere, and what is grace other than the presence of God, of God's love? Then when the Vatican Council II reminded us of the centrality of the Eucharist in our spiritual lives, my appreciation of the Mass opened up. In the Constitution on the Sacred Liturgy, the Church fathers wrote (article 10), "The liturgy (the Mass) is the summit toward which the activity of the Church is directed, at the same time it is the fountain from which all her power flows." That meant to me that I had, even as a seminarian, missed the richness of the Mass. I believed (and still believe!) that Jesus is physically present in the Mass, that the Holy Spirit, when invoked by the ordained priest, changes the bread and wine on the altar into the body and blood of Jesus, and that participation in this Eucharistic feast gives us nourishment while also joining us into one body across the world as the people of God. In other words, the Mass is an act of love. Again, in the words of Vatican II, "From the liturgy then, and especially from the Eucharist, grace [*God's love*] is poured forth upon us as from a fountain."

I am convinced that the Church, with its emphasis on Jesus's crucifixion and St. Paul's use of the idea of that sacrifice ransoming mankind from the curse of sin, has obscured the profound gift of love that is the essence of the Mass (just as it is God's essence). The incarnation where Jesus took on our flesh and participated fully in our humanity is not only an unspeakable mystery; it is also the miracle of love. God turns the tables. Having created man and woman in the image of God, God now becomes the image of man/woman. He comes to save us from ourselves by showing and teaching us how to love. His murder is the ultimate expression of love since he gave up his life to help us understand the power of love. His resurrection is the proof of his divinity, but the incarnation is the overwhelming gift. Yet there is another message there: love may demand a terrible price, but love can make paying that price acceptable and a chance to bestow a gift.

When I began to ponder those insights into "God is love" and "grace is everywhere" and "the only person who truly has joy is one who lives in love" (Thomas Aquinas), I recognized how the Mass is actually a dialogue of love. Far from being an obligation, it is an invitation to join in a celebratory feast with fellow lovers. That is why it is important for us laypeople to be active participants in the sacred liturgy because we are there as lovers. Aquinas also teaches us that "fear is the beginning of despair just as hope is the beginning of daring." Thus, we do not come to Mass in fear. Aquinas again said, "Inordinate fear is included in every sin"—and ours is a culture of fear. We come in hope. Hope bursts forth from love, and in this festive event of the Mass, we not only bring our love, but we are filled with hope. No, more than that. We are filled with the confidence and the conviction that God will see us and hear us. We dare to bring our gift of ourselves while we come to receive the gift of divine life in the sacrament of love.

The Mass is a communal experience that begins with our coming together as a community, as sharers in this wondrous mystery. In songs, we praise our Creator-Teacher-Sanctifier; we ask forgiveness from our loving God for our weaknesses and shortcomings, our selfishness, and our lack of caring for others. Then we listen to God's Word and its further exposition in a homily. We respond to that with our requests for support and our affirmation of our belief in the God of love. Then we offer ourselves to God using the symbol of money to reflect the generosity of our hearts. God then, in a mysterious, beyond understanding miracle, comes to us in the form of bread and wine and feeds us. As he does so, we are reminded of his words at his last supper with his disciples: "As my father loves me, so I also love you. Remain in my love . . . This is my commandment: love one another as I love you . . . You are my friends if you do what I command you" (John 15: 9, 12, 14). Then we feast together in joy, sing praises to this God of wild love and reckless giving, receive his blessing and his commission to go forth, and change the world from fear to love. So long as I can keep

THOMAS W. MAHAN

that process in mind, the Mass becomes a daring and exciting experience; otherwise, it is old hat and empty.

I mentioned above my conviction that we have overplayed the "ransom from the bonds of sin" card so that the trump card of "God is love" has been obscured. For me, it is hard to find salvation in the midst of guilt. Salvation is a gift; it is not earned. God's love for me does not depend upon my not committing adultery or killing; it is my love of God (and wife) that keeps me from those acts. In other words, my efforts toward living the way of love that Jesus taught is my *gift* because my relationship with Jesus stems from love. Sometimes, my ego and competing desires may impede that love, and I fall short of my intent. Paul tells us that "the spirit indeed is willing, but the flesh is weak." To me, that means that my love of self (and that includes comfort, pleasure, excitement, material goods, etc.) has interfered with my love of Jesus.

How does that happen? Maybe a discussion of what St. Augustine called original sin, passed down almost genetically from Adam and Eve to human beings, would be appropriate here. I, of course, have already mentioned my trouble with that concept since I am convinced that the story of Adam and Eve is not historical. It is an allegory to teach a lesson. It tells us, in my understanding, that the Creator loved us so much that s/he granted us freedom of choice—free will—and also gave us the intelligence to discover when we have made poor choices. When Adam and Eve covered themselves with fig leaves, they hoped (unrealistically!) that they could cover their misstep and hide it from God. How well that symbolizes the ease with which we humans slip into deceit, blaming others (poor Eve!) and covering up rather than admitting our errors or shortcomings. What Augustine called original sin is something more profound; it is the acknowledgment that God, in her/his wisdom, created us free in a world filled with wonders (and dangers) that may distract us from God and God's Word. God's love and God's trust are the gifts that make it possible for us to ignore, abandon, or reject the divine. Thomas Aquinas (you may have guessed that he is one of my favorite authors) writes that "sacred writings are bound in two volumes—that of creation and that of Holy Scripture." In other words, all around us nature (and especially human nature) shouts the goodness and greatness of God, which is also attested in the Bible. Yet that same nature (again including human nature!) can either proclaim God's presence or lead us to indulge our own ego. With God's gift of free will, we who have ears can refuse to hear, and we with eyes can refuse to see.

If you remember the quote from Thomas Wolfe in the early pages of this manuscript, perhaps you can agree with my interpretation of Wolfe's words as his sense that God's love and the call to follow that example of love is too much of a burden. It is better to reject Christ even though we may keep some trappings of Christianity than to become a lover of God in others. The strange fact is that for true lovers, there is no burden in caring for and giving to those loved. In a very real sense, it is a privilege to have the opportunity to translate inner feelings into outer actions. Love, when not ensnared in love of self, takes us out of ourselves and places us in joyful service to others. There is often a price to this love (look at Jesus!), but it is never anger or self-pity or resentment. When Virgil wrote that "love conquers all things," he was unknowingly a prophet of the Christ-message.

When we say that Christianity (or the Christ-message) is countercultural, that is, most dramatically true when we recognize the pervasive culture of fear that has infected the world compared with the Jesus-message (in word and action) of the way of love. The Jesus story does not have what the world would call a happy ending nor do we have any promise that our embrace of Jesus's example of love at any cost will bring us rewards in the eyes of the world. In fact, the promise seems almost opposite when Jesus tells us in Luke's Gospel (6:22), "Blessed are you when people hate you, and when they exclude and insult you, and denounce your name as evil, on account of the Son of Man." I suspect that only lovers can drink that cup. Fear carries with it the infection of suspicion and paranoia. It destroys openness and casts aside forgiveness and acceptance. It limits compassion to one's own and breeds contempt and hate for those who are different. Again, in the words of Aquinas, "Fear is included in every sin." We can see the sin permeating our fear-cursed world hidden in such actions as homeschooling, in the exploitation of immigrant workers, in the effort to deny illegal immigrants basic human rights, in the adoption of preventive acts of war, in the reduction of support for the needy and aged, in the efforts to sabotage support for safety networks for the seriously ill and unemployed, as well as the efforts to close down quality educational opportunities for much of our citizenry. All those current trends reject Jesus's way of love.

Those who spoke of a cultural war were close to the truth, but they misperceived the opponents. The war is between the culture of fear and the way of love, between the armored gladiators of what's best for number 1 and the naked lovers of all of God's creation.

SANCTITY, SEX, AND SIN

THOSE ARE THREE fairly simple words, but they can conjure up a wide range of perceptions. In posing that title as I have, I want to explore how those three concepts relate to each other—perhaps even how they influence each other. The dictionary tells us that "sanctity" and "holiness" are synonyms, but "sanctity" made for an alliterative title. Vatican II in the *Dogmatic Constitution on the Church* (*Lumen Gentium*, para. 40) makes clear that all the faithful are called to holiness but that the call will be answered in many different ways. In the *New Dictionary of Catholic Spirituality*, the author of the article on holiness, Notre Dame professor Lawrence Cunningham, stresses that holiness is a relationship and, for the Christian, a relationship with Jesus. There is no one road to holiness as there is no one form of expressing love. Holiness is our choice of how to be with Christ in this world and our responsible follow-through on that choice.

St. Teresa of Avila, the sixteenth-century mystic and religious activist-reformer and first woman given the title of "doctor of the Church," wrote, "From silly devotions and sour-faced saints, good Lord, deliver us." So holiness is not tied to piety nor to somberness; it is a commitment and a process of living that commitment. Perhaps St. Ignatius of Loyola, founder of the Jesuits, gives us some useful advice that can steer us in answering this call to holiness. Ignatius writes, "Seek the presence of God in all things: in conversation, in walking, in looking, in tasting, in hearing, in understanding, and in all that we do, since it is a fact that his [Jesus's] divine majesty is everywhere by his presence, power and essence." In other words, holiness is an attitude and a style of living; it is not an achievement. Nor does it require heroic actions. It does require a love relationship, which leads us to proclaim the fact Jesus stated in John's Gospel: people will know that we are his followers by the fact that we love one another.

That quick overview of holiness brings us to the topic of sex. Sex has been a central concern for Church writers and spokesmen through the two millennia of its existence. We have had trouble reconciling the desires of the body (and sexual desires seem to have been a larger problem than desires for food or drink) and the life of the spirit. In fact, some of the early heresies denied that Jesus really had a physical body; it just appeared that way. The insistence of many Church leaders that Mary, mother of Jesus, retained her virginal status throughout her life reflected the perception that human sexual activity that might lead to pregnancy would have been demeaning for God's mother (even though God had created sex and sexual desire). The writers of the Gnostic gospels along with the writers of the *Gospel of Thomas* and the *Acts of Thomas* show a disdain for the material world, especially the human body.

Earlier I referred to the letter of Pope St. Gregory the Great who died in 604 and whose papacy was marked by many reform initiatives. That letter expressed the deep reservations that existed in regard to sexual activity when he stated that it was sinful (though only a venial sin) for married couples to find any pleasure in the conjugal act. This natural behavior, designed by the Creator and necessary for the continuation of the human race, was tainted unless it was an act done out of duty with no pleasure connected with it. How different is the modern post-Vatican II Church, which sees sexual behavior as a part of the gift in marriage that supports the bond of love.

I join those who go even further. I believe that the sexual union is an almost unique avenue for discovering the ecstasy of love that reaches the human pinnacle of closeness to God in its total, uncontrolled sharing, its openness and vulnerability, its ultimate giving of self with no limitations. Mystics, such as Teresa of Avila, who have experiences of an intense union with God, use language similar to that which describes intense, passionate, love-driven sex. I have to admit that my hero, Thomas Aquinas, worried about this lack of rational control that accompanies such intense, passionate behaviors. For him, lack of rational control was a dangerous experience similar to becoming drunk. So here, as well as on his view of women as lower on the scale of humanity than males, I have to part company with Thomas. However, he does redeem himself some when he writes as cited earlier, "No one can live without delight and that is why a person deprived of spiritual joy seeks carnal pleasures." For me, the idea that we all need delight is another sign of God's bountiful gifts. And sex, I propose, is an avenue where both spiritual joy and carnal pleasure can come together.

Of course, not all sex, even not all married sex, is rooted in spiritual awareness. Those times are precious and unique as are the experiences of mystics. But sex in its ordinary form can be a significant component of a healthy marital relationship; it can also be a destructive factor. Like all human desires or appetites, we can abuse and/or exploit them. At the same time, the realm of sexual behavior seems to attract an inordinate amount of attention from theologians and ecclesiastics. Seminary courses in moral theology seem to find the sixth and ninth commandments a rich topic for discussing human weaknesses and foibles. Under the heading of sin, we will return to that aspect of sex, but now I want to explore the three aspects of human sexual behavior that I feel need to be opened to some broader analysis than a simple condemnation. They are the use of artificial methods of preventing pregnancy, the current and apparently growing use of cohabitation as a prelude to, or substitute for, marriage and same-sex unions.

Even though the Church, since Vatican II, has modified its teaching on the purpose of marriage by raising, as its first mentioned purpose, "the good of the spouses" rather than having that purpose secondary to the procreation of children (*Catechism,* para. 1660; *Code of Canon Law,* para. 1055), there remains a lot of concern about sexual behavior. Modern industrial culture along with the concern for the dignity of persons, especially married women, has made the incidence of large numbers of children no longer a measure of a couple's faith and devotion to the Church. Health, economic, and psychological concerns as well as the commitment to provide for each child the opportunities for full development has made the limitation and spacing of children not only acceptable but accepted. The Church itself in its local parishes has often sponsored sessions on natural family planning, which provides information on reducing (if not, eliminating) the probability of pregnancy resulting from sexual activity. In other words, there is a Church-authorized approach to contraception that does not require abstinence.

When Blessed Pope John XXIII convoked the Second Vatican Council, he was aware of the growing questions about other (called artificial) methods of contraception. To provide him guidance, he appointed a papal commission made of laymen and laywomen as well as clergy to study this issue made more pressing by the development of the contraceptive pill that chemically controlled ovulation. John XXIII died, and his successor, Pope Paul VI, continued the commission. He also indicated to the bishops assembled to deliberate issues in the council that he was reserving to himself any teachings on the legitimacy of contraceptive use. The commission majority recommended to Paul that the Church modify its absolute ban on artificial methods of contraception and recognize new approaches such as the pill as legitimate for the faithful to use. After some study, Paul issued his encyclical "Humanae Vitae," which reaffirmed the traditional Church position against any and all artificial contraceptives. This provoked a sense of disappointment on a wide basis, including among some bishops and clergy. The theology faculty at my alma mater (The Catholic University of America) signed a petition supporting the use of contraceptives like the pill. Until the pedophile scandal, "Humanae Vitae" provoked an unequalled injury to the credibility of the teaching authority of the Church.

At the heart of this crisis is the fact that those using the so-called natural method and those using the pejoratively labeled artificial method have the same intent: prevention of pregnancy. Neither is absolutely foolproof, but the probability of error is somewhat greater with the natural method, and that method is more burdensome. Given that intent is a very important component of moral behavior, many (including this author who, because of age, has no personal investment in the issue) wonder at this ruling. My wonder leads me to the hypothesis that the approval of strategies even including those such as the pill that do not create a physical barrier to insemination might seem like the Church has changed its mind. Maybe further consideration would lead the Church to add the allowance of contraceptive methods as it decided after centuries to allow the charging of interest on loans and finally banned slavery in all its forms. Change is not a sign of weakness.

Our second issue has to do with what is euphemistically, if awkwardly, called cohabitation. That term to me already sounds negative, and I prefer the more neutral phrase "living together." It may not surprise most readers that the Church does not have nice things to say about that practice. The Catechism (para. 2390-2391) discusses what it calls free unions (para. 2390) and trial marriages (para. 2391); in both cases, it says "no" except that the "no" is louder in regard to long-term relationships without the benefit of marriage. The prohibition of such unions is direct and clear: "The sexual act must take place exclusively within marriage" (para. 2390). The Catechism, when dealing with living together as a prelude to marriage, worries about the danger of change of mind or straying to another liaison, etc., summing up the discussion with "human love does not tolerate 'trial marriages'" (para. 2391). Despite the fact that the Church (at least in the so-called Latin rite) sees the man and the woman as the ministers of the sacrament of matrimony, apparently those ministers cannot convey the blessings of grace upon themselves without a Church witness (priest or deacon).

I have already offered my opinion that when love dies, so does the marriage. The couple and the rest of society may pretend that the marriage still exists, but that is a cruel deception (probably cruelest because it is a self-deception). Often economics and habit are the factors that lead such couples to live the make-believe relationship, sometimes with and sometimes without sex. Now I wonder if a marriage exists de facto where the man and the woman are united in love and with the intent to share their lives together. States have recognized what is sometimes called a common-law marriage. Where there is passionate love combined with trust, respect, and commitment to each other, there is the environment for marriage and the setting for grace.

Our third topic is perhaps the most controversial of the three: same-sex marriage. Before we can reasonably discuss that issue, we have to come to grips with our understanding of homosexuality. I recall when I was a clinical psychology intern in a large state-operated mental hospital, homosexuality, both overt and covert, was considered to be a psychiatric illness. To many, regardless of overt behavior, it was a perversion. Times have changed some. The evidence now is clear that for the majority of gays and lesbians, there is an innate orientation toward the same sex. That orientation is not a choice; it is intrinsic to her or his being. Nonetheless, many gay and lesbian individuals experience themselves as exiles—cut off from family, neighbors, and even the Church. This disconnect between their created reality and the isolation/rejection stemming from the treatment of others can thwart the development of a sense of basic trust—trust in the world as well as trust in others—that Erik Erikson posed as foundational to the evolution of a healthy sense of self. In this sense, lesbians and gays come early to the challenge of discovering and accepting themselves. Part of that acceptance is the awareness of their longing for the intimate relationship, which is the quest of all human beings.

While the Church counsels acceptance and compassion for lesbians and gays (*Catechism*, para. 2357-2359), the *Catechism* also plainly states that "homosexual acts are intrinsically disordered" and, quoting from the 1975 declaration of the Congregation for the Doctrine of the Faith, "Persona Humana," goes on to describe the homosexual orientation as "objectively disordered." These persons are thus "called to chastity." They did not volunteer it; they are, in my words, condemned, more than called, to it. It is one thing for the man about to be ordained to embrace celibacy as his gift to his God. It is quite another to be told that God somehow has selected lesbians and gays to be doomed to never experience the passionate, intimate relationship, which seems so clearly to be the divine intent without offending the Creator.

Some of the tactics used by our American bishops to combat the growing acceptance of legally sanctioned same-sex partnerships seem to be straight out of the "culture of fear" agenda. I know of no data to support the claim that same-sex couples who serve as parents for children are less effective or have children with more problems than adopted children in straight families. I cannot fathom how anyone can see in the public endorsement of gay/lesbian partnerships a threat to the concept of marriage. I seriously doubt that those of us who are heterosexually oriented will suddenly convert to homosexual relationships. Of all the current moral issues, same-sex marriage seems the one most attractive to red herrings.

The real issue is, can love that is faithful, respectful, trusting, and passionate be good only between heterosexual couples? It is true that the same-sex couples cannot beget children as the fruit of their love, but then there are numbers of heterosexual couples who have the same limitation and the Church does not restrict marriage only to those of childbearing age. Once more, I find myself wondering if at some future date we will recognize that this kind of love comes from God and our acceptance of it is in accord with Jesus's way of love.

In all three of these examples of issues surrounding human sexual behavior, we have been skirting the topic of *sin*. What is sin? Many have been introduced to sin as a breaking of the rules, a transgression of the law. In fact, we were instructed to report the number of transgressions in our confessions; it was seen as a case of black-and-white. Doubts crept into that model when we found that some laws changed and the sin disappeared—for example, the Church law about abstinence from meat on Fridays prior to Vatican II. *The New Dictionary of Catholic Spirituality*, in one of the longer articles in the volume, offers a more stable and more personal definition: sin is a betrayal of a relationship with God. Sin threatens the health of the bond between us, me personally and us as a community, and the God of wild love and reckless giving. Another way of phrasing my view of sin is to see it as listening to our ego rather than our heart—ignoring our commitment to love God and our neighbor. Sin is selfishness. It is placing myself and my wants/impulses above all other concerns. I become my own god, which may well be another lesson from the Adam and Eve story—they replaced God.

Of course, there are very differing degrees of this pattern of behavior, but our culture, with its emphasis on material goods and on the individual being number 1, creates a climate where it is easy to slip into such behaviors without much awareness. That is why those who feel that God is distant, who do not sense that "grace is everywhere," may slide easily into what we call sin—into behaviors that disrupt our connection to the God of wild love and reckless giving.

As I have noted, Thomas Aquinas tells us that all sin has the component of inordinate fear. Given that our Western world, perhaps the entire planet, is living in and reacting to this culture of fear, are there some pervasive influences that are particularly disruptive of our being free to embrace the God of love? I would nominate five basic sins as signs of our loss of a sense of the presence of the divine in our daily world. The most dangerous and most corrupting is the sin of *fear*. Fear drives out love; it is, in fact, the opposite of love. Since God is love and we, as images of God, must reflect love, the most dangerous influence impacting our pursuit of holiness on our becoming whole and holy persons is the presence of fear in our lives. I am aware of the biblical phrase "fear of God," which I see as a way of expressing awe when we contemplate the divine. I am using fear as an emotion that closes us up and creates not just a foreboding but a closing off of our ability to be open to the world. It is the enemy of trust and poisons faith founded on love. One of the marks of the corruption of our world is the use of fear in political campaigns where the unspoken message is that it is acceptable to hurt others so that you will be safer. The fact that history suggests the opposite does not bother those who develop and disseminate such fears. And the fact that most believers do not see the contradiction between that message and Jesus's way of love shows how ingrained fear is throughout our culture.

Related to fear, and frequently a consequence of fear, is the sin of *deceit*. This includes that most insidious form of deceit—self-deception. Deceit, like fear, is rampant in our society, and it is not a new phenomenon. In the allegory of Adam and Eve, we find the fearful couple grasping for fig leaves to hide the bare facts of what they had done. I must admit that I have wondered for decades how they attached the fig leaves to cover their physical nakedness, but the story is really about their effort to avoid responsibility for their actions of disobedience by hiding and blaming—Adam blaming the woman, and Eve blaming the serpent. In our daily lives, we find that governments, corporations, and organizations as well as individuals (including many of us!) embrace deceit rather than acknowledge the truth about ourselves and/or what we have done. Alas, even the Church in the ongoing pedophile scandal has used deceit to cover up some of its unpleasant actions. Our egos, whether personal or corporate, whether secular or religious, resist being exposed as engaging in wrongful actions.

So we try to hide by way of deceit. As with Adam and Eve, our shame that we try to hide under fig leaves or masks is much more injurious to us and our reputations than our naked honesty would have been.

The user of deceit behaves as if image is more important than reality. Deceit is motivated by fear, shows disrespect and scorn for those whom the person or the organization hopes to deceive, falls back on lies, and undermines trust. As an example in personal lives, the negative impact of adultery has nothing to do with sex. It has to do with deceit, with lying, and with disrespect for loved ones, family, friends, and colleagues, and it destroys bonds of trust so essential in love relationships. Yet how easy it is to fall into deceit. Children learn to cover up actions out of fear; adults in varying situations will adapt their stories to make themselves look better according to what they sense will work. Many, if not most, of us have secrets that we would prefer to keep hidden, and if there is a danger of discovery, we turn to various deceitful techniques. In addition to the basic fig leaves, we develop a number of different masks to help us put forth an image when it is the naked self that would protect us most in God's eyes.

The third sin that I see as a vicious curse in our society is *greed*. The *Catechism* (para. 1866) tells us that the sin of greed, unlike fear and deceit, is included in the list of capital sins that go back to St. John Cassian (fourth century CE) and St. Gregory the Great (sixth century CE) where it goes under the title of *avarice*. The word "greed" to my mind has a stronger Anglo-Saxon bluntness than the Latin-based "avarice" and is a familiar term in today's conversation, so I will write of the sin of greed. We even have heard the slogan, "Greed is good," turning the world upside down by indicating that sin is virtue. What makes greed a sin and one so destructive in the twenty-first century? Greed is the exemplar of our placing ourselves and our wants first, even to the detriment of our neighbors/strangers. As Jesus made very clear and as he is echoed in both the letters of St. James and St. John, the love of God is intertwined with our love or neighbor and of enemy.

Perhaps even more important is that greed distorts our values and puts ourselves above God. Through greed, we are seduced into seeking to save a few dollars by advocating to have our taxes cut even though that reduction would mean others would lose various forms of assistance. This placing of self above the common good is a greed-oriented pattern. So too is the exploitation of migrant workers or cheating on one's income tax or the building of a magnificent home, far beyond one's needs, just because one has the resources to do so. Unfortunately, greed is so pervasive in our society that we often do not recognize its presence or influence. I have joked for years about expecting that my children might want to give me a Bentley automobile as a Christmas gift, but I know that I would be too embarrassed to be seen driving it. In fact, I wonder if the very manufacture of vehicles such as the Bentley or the Rolls-Royce or the Maserati is not sinful. When there is so much hunger and homelessness in the world, can the expenditure of hundreds of thousands of dollars on one car be justified?

Of course, that example lets me off the hook. There is no chance that my children are going to give me such a car. But what are the things that I do or buy in my life that exceed the justification of a mild, occasional luxury? Surely, the goods of this world are intended for our pleasure and enjoyment, but when do I pass beyond giving glory to God in the use and enjoyment of creation to an acquisitive style that feeds itself? I suspect that each of us must decide for ourselves where that line is drawn, where the pleasure of the material world, whether a Bentley or a filet mignon or a highly rated bottle of wine blinds us to the fact that we owe the God of wild love and reckless giving, glory, praise, and thanks for such gifts. I will go a step further and question whether anyone can justify the multimillion-dollar salaries of professional athletes and of corporate CEOs. In the 1950s when Bob Cousy, the outstanding guard on the Boston Celtics basketball team, was earning about $25,000 at the height of his career, my father, a school superintendent in a medium-sized New England city, was earning about $15,000. Today, the superintendent in such a city might be earning $150,000, but the star player on a team in the NBA might be paid $10,000,000 or more. So too the CEO of a major corporation will often have an annual income in those figures.

I am not in favor of socialism, which has become a pejorative term in the political arena. Nonetheless, there seems to me to be no question that the disparity of income and other compensation for those at the top of the organizational hierarchy compared with the people who do the actual work to make those organizations successful is shameful, if not immoral. The fact that those facts are simply business as usual testifies to how blind we have become about greed and how Jesus's message is ignored even as his name is invoked.

The fourth major sin, which is often coupled with both greed and deceit, is *pride*. It too is listed as one of the capital sins, and it certainly has earned its place there. It has a significant overlap in today's terminology with "ego" even though the term "ego" seems to lack a connotation of sin or of cutting one off from the divine. Pride is not to be confused with healthy self-esteem nor with awareness and gratitude for talents or skills or gifts. Pride in one's work is not sinful nor is the desire to have one's accomplishments acknowledged and appreciated. What is sinful is the pushing of oneself forward, of presuming to be the expert, of putting others down, and of hiding one's mistakes. I must admit that when I hear some of my peers talk about their grandchildren's accomplishments, I wonder if that might be bordering on the sinful. You will note that I said "grandchildren" and not "children" since I have no grandchildren and thus can *with pride* excuse myself from that danger. Seriously though, pride easily leads to deceit and to a need to be appreciated that ignores others and may be out of proportion. Pride that leads to actions that are directly hurtful to others whether by an individual, an organization, or a nation fall under the category of sin. Pride is seen in the need to be first, in the need to take over and be heard, in the need to win at all costs, in the insatiable need for approval, and in the physical signs of that approval. A more subtle kind of pride, also part of the sin of pride, is an unwillingness to accept help and an independence that rejects all efforts to provide support. At the root of pride is the *fear* that I or my organization or my country will be discovered or seen to be less effective or powerful or talented than I think I deserve to be. In other words, pride leads me to put myself above others and often to ignore the God of love.

The fifth and final of what I call the sins that are a curse in our culture is *anger*. Anger is another of the capital sins recognized early in the Church. I feel strongly that anger is always a negative emotion, even when it is the source of motivation to correct an evil situation. People frequently cite Jesus's driving the money changers from the temple as an example of righteous anger. I find no translation of that episode from either Greek or Latin sources that mentions that Jesus was angry, so I continue to say that anger is always a negative emotion, which can lead to positive action, but at a price. The price is that anger inevitably constricts our openness and directs our awareness to a target that is devalued in our eyes. Flowing from that anger may come strife, slander, gossip, insult, public punishment, sarcasm, indignation, revenge/getting even, and physical acting out as well as disservice to one's own physical health. Anger can take many forms, some direct and others indirect. Listed above are some of the direct forms, but the indirect ones can often be equally, if not more, hurtful. For example, passive aggression where the angry person never directly expresses her/his anger but punishes the object of anger and, frequently, other innocent bystanders, by withdrawal or by avoiding discussion or by slowing down work is a common form of anger expression. One of the many dangers of anger is its potential for creating anger in others; it is a very contagious sin. As an antidote to the use of anger, we need to listen again to Blessed Pope John XXIII's words as he addressed the opening session of Vatican II: "But today we prefer to make use of the medicine of mercy rather than that of severity."

Those five sins are, in my estimation, the sins that feed the culture of fear in which we live. They all, alone and together, create the godless society which permeates our world. Just as love drives out fear, so also fear drives out love. All five of these human reactions disrupt relationships and directly undermine the trust and respect, which are foundations for forgiveness, acceptance, compassion, and love. Fear, deceit, and greed are at the heart of our addictive society with addictions to power, money, and fame. What makes these five reactions so destructive is that they have infected our governments, our institutions, and our corporations. Not even my church, which I love and admire, has escaped the scourge—nor have I. I look at my life, and I see how I have fallen into each of those five, but I will not burden any reader with a more detailed confession.

As I look at my church, fear has reared its ugly presence in many forms. Restricting my purview to recent times, I note the attacks on the media as being anti-Catholic and the fear-mongering that legislative approval of same-sex marriages may destroy the family. When it comes to deceit, need we go further than the cover-up of the pedophile scandal? I give the Church a better score on greed, though its real estate and art holdings in an age of so much hunger and homelessness are troublesome. Pride seems almost inevitable when the Church's teaching demands its acceptance as the voice of Jesus even when the voice seems alien to Jesus's message. In some instances, the Church has softened that pride by reinterpreting statements that seem overly officious. Examples of those statements are the following: "Error has no rights" (so why open dialogue with other faiths?) and "Outside the Church, there is no salvation" (softened by Vatican II documents that saw the Church as broader than the institutional organization). One of the avenues for expressing anger is to cut people off and to punish them. The bishops who have indicated their intent to deny the sacraments to politicians who refuse to vote against their consciences are showing anger as is the bishop of Phoenix, Thomas J. Olmsted, in his excommunication of Sister Margaret Mary whom he accuses of allowing a direct abortion and his subsequent stripping of St. Joseph Hospital, where she worked, of the use of the word "Catholic" in describing itself.

I could, of course, have a much richer pool of examples to draw upon if I were to try to give illustrations from the government of the United States or any other nation. I have no doubt that if I had knowledge of the history of different churches or religious groups, I could also find these five sins endemic. I chose to use my church because it exemplifies for me the humanness that Jesus came to give divine status. The Church, like the people of God, is subject to the culture even though it is called to be a countercultural force. The important issue is that the Church—my church—needs forgiveness, acceptance, compassion, and love just as does the people of God. The Church exists because of sinfulness, because our quest for wholeness/holiness is never complete, and it is the beacon of light leading us to awareness that grace is everywhere.

The reader may note that I have not included any sexual behaviors in this category of the five most dangerous sins of our time. That is intentional. The sins against the sixth and ninth commandments have, I think, been given a life of their own that masks the real source of their being disruptive of human and the human-divine relationships. I certainly do not deny the power and attractiveness of human sexuality, but to color it sinful obscures the fact that sexual union can be a source of grace and a premonition of the ecstasy of being in the presence of the divine.

The abuse of sex—rape, sexual molestation, incest, and exploitation—are serious offenses, but at their core, they are acts that stem from fear, greed, and anger. Behaviors such as adultery are disruptive of human relations because they are usually based in deceit, and they involve the breaking of a covenant. In most cases of extramarital sex, the participants are placing their desires before the good of others and thus placing self-love above all else. Even so, I see the behaviors and addictions that flow from my five most dangerous sins as the source of corruption that permeates our culture. Sex can be an avenue, inappropriate to be sure, for at least, a temporary escape from the culture of fear into a temporary discovery of pleasure. The same is true for many other escape avenues: food, alcohol, sleep, work, shopping, etc. My comments in an earlier section point out how, in my mind, the prohibition of some sexual behaviors may be less important and less relevant with the cultural changes in the roles of women.

Let me close this section with a reminder that sin is a failure to live the two great commandments: to love God and to love our neighbor (defined as everybody). Everything in this world is essentially good; how we use and/

or relate to those goods, including ourselves, determines the morality of our thoughts and actions. My wife Susan recently brought to my attention an article entitled "Neurons of Compassion" by Arizona State University professor Allan J. Hamilton, MD. In that article, which appeared in the September-October 2009 issue of *Spirituality & Health,* Dr. Hamilton quotes from a memoir by G. M. Gilbert who was a psychologist-observer at the Nuremberg trials after World War II. Gilbert sums up his study and analysis of the war criminals with this statement: "*Evil, I think, is the absence of empathy.*" That sounds to me like a modern confirmation of Aquinas's teaching that "evil is the absence of good."

We are all blessed by the fact that *grace is everywhere*; every part of our bodies, every appetite that we have, every person, and every object in the world, animate and inanimate—all are potential sources of grace. Because we have free will and because we have the freedom to ignore or reject those two fundamental commandments, all these same gifts of potential grace can be turned into occasions of sin. In religious education classes, the term "occasion of sin" was common as a warning about the dangers of the world. In this twenty-first century where God seems so distant, if even existing, to many people, we need to emphasize *occasions of grace*. Every minute of our every day is filled with the occasions of grace. We need to train our awareness to sense them and embrace them.

GUIDES TO HOLINESS: FOUR GOSPEL THEMES

S OME FIFTEEN YEARS ago, I ran across a volume that helped me sort through the various messages contained in the New Testament writings. The book, *The Moral Vision of the New Testament* (New York: Harper-Collins, 1996) written by Duke University professor, R. B. Hays, stirred my grappling with the issue of what the essential messages of those canonical writings are. I have already underlined my belief that the basic Jesus-message is *love*. Love, indeed, is God's essence, and our being created in God's image means that love is central to our being. For me, all the rest of Jesus's teachings are derived from the twin aspects of the love commandments. Professor Hays, however, takes a somewhat different tack. He is looking at the entire New Testament canon and finds that there are writings where love is not a central theme (cf. pp. 200-203) and cannot be construed to be the synthesizing factor in some major writings, specifically, *Mark's Gospel, Acts, Romans,* and *Revelation.* Nonetheless, Hays does list three focal images, which I have found very helpful: community, cross, and new creation. For my purposes, I have translated "new creation" into "conversion" and have added a fourth theme of nonviolence.

In my view, all four of these themes—*community, conversion, cross, and nonviolence/forgiveness*—are directly descended from love. As Hays makes clear in his writing, the early Church, reflected in the writings of some of the New Testament authors, began to shift focus from love to power and control. I do not doubt the accuracy of that perception based upon our history of the Christian churches through the ages. Certainly today, as I hope has been set forth in the earlier pages of this monograph, we continue to struggle between the prophets of love and the defenders of the organization, which will disintegrate without attention to control and power. The critical issue for my church can be summed up in that dialectic: how to balance the message of love, of inclusivity, and of universal salvation with the need for rules, for standards, for order, and for correctness in interpreting the Jesus phenomenon. That is no easy job! Over time, the pendulum seems to swing more toward one direction, then toward the other. I will offer no plan to resolve that dynamic though I believe that the control-power orientation will corrupt the Jesus-message unless that segment of the people of God is suffused with the spirit of love.

I want to ignore, at least for a while, that dialectic and look at the four basic themes, which I am convinced are central to the Jesus-message of love. I will deal with them in the order listed above, which is also their alphabetical order.

Community

When I was growing up in the 1930s and 1940s, the concept of the community as the heart of the Christian life escaped me. Even when, as a teenager in the 1940s, I became aware of the teaching on the Church as the mystical body of Christ, I saw myself as an individual combined with other individuals in that mystical body, not as interdependent members. The phrase "the people of God" used in the Vatican II literature opened up a whole new understanding. The connection with the Judaic "chosen people" concept was almost inevitable but with a striking difference. The people of God was expansive; it potentially included all people—deceased, alive, and yet to come. The use of the term "saints" by St. Paul to describe the believers with all their weaknesses and sins now made sense and gave a different depth to my belief in the "communion of saints" as referring to all who have struggled or are still struggling to attain wholeness/holiness.

The reference above to the Jewish sense of being the chosen people brought with it an awareness of two features that are central to the Jewish understanding of being the chosen people. There is, in Jewish tradition, both a component of justice and of mercy, but those English words are weak translations for what the Hebrew words connote. "Justice," in this context, has been defined as "a loving concern that all people have what is needed for a decent, fulfilling human life . . . and is not 'merely' legal." (cf. "Community" in *The New Dictionary of Catholic Spirituality*). The same writer (Bernard Lee, SM) emphasizes that the word "mercy" does not convey the richer sense of the Hebrew, which may be better translated as "extraordinary compassion."

Jesus uses many images to bring forth the reality of community in his teachings and actions. He uses metaphors such as the vine and branches and the good shepherd and sheep, but the most telling is his use of the word "father" to refer to God the Creator and his telling his disciples, his friends, that no one comes to the Father except through him. Coupled with those images and statements is Jesus's comment that people will know his followers by how they love one another. As I look back to my perceptions up through the 1950s, I become aware of how limited and barren was my spiritual insight. I went to Mass frequently, most weeks at least two or three times, but at Mass, I focused on *my* reading in my daily missal and paid little attention to (and definitely never conversed with) those sitting around me. Even then, the title "celebrant" struck me as strange: a man with his back to me, mumbling in Latin and whose sermon was mostly likely intended to evoke fear of eternal damnation, struck me as a very inappropriate way to celebrate.

The people of God are now the celebrants with the priest presiding at the feast. That image fits much better with the Jesus whom I perceive as I read the Gospels, and the priest, as another Christ, who becomes a leader of the "royal priesthood" of the baptized, female and male, as they celebrate and participate in the feast of love and thanksgiving. Community becomes both the source of and the calling to holiness. Just as love is the essence of God, so love is the essence of human holiness. That love is discovered and expressed in the community. The new covenant is not between Jesus/God and me. By baptism, I am entered into the community, into the people of God, and into the covenant that God has with that community where the Church plays the role—sometimes with integrity, sometimes somewhat corrupted by human tendencies—as the voice and the guardian of the wisdom of the way of love. As Chicago priest and former seminary professor, Louis J. Cameli, writes, "We go to God together." Cameli, in his introduction to his little book, *Going to God Together,* quotes a Jesuit professor who said, "*The [Vatican II] council fathers preferred to talk about being incorporated into the Church rather than to talk about membership in the Church. We do not just belong to the Church, but we become the Church.*"

That means that we move from being a passive member concerned about our personal salvation to an active part of the Church, of the march of all creation toward life in Jesus. The test of that change lies in our commitment to work to bring about the kingdom that Jesus often spoke about. Holiness goes beyond piety and the Ten Commandments; it is demonstrated in forgiveness of all, including enemies, of acceptance of all, of compassion toward all, and of love for all. That is not easy for us humans with our egos and our sense of identity with groups and our desire to protect ourselves and our loved ones.

So how do we go about creating these communities of love, the communities that reflect the Jesus-message? M. Scott Peck, author of the longtime best seller *The Road Less Travelled* and many other volumes, established with his then wife Lily the Foundation for Community Encouragement. This was a response to their perceived breakdown of

THOMAS W. MAHAN

the sense of community in the United States. From their experience in that undertaking, they discerned four stages in community development: pseudocommunity, chaos, emptiness, and community. We all have been part of pseudocommunities. These are those get-togethers where we chat, shake hands, wish everybody well, and then go each our own way. In most situations, that is what the Sunday Mass or other religious service is. It becomes almost impossible to convert such a gathering, especially if it involves more than thirty people, directly into a sustainable community. For a brief time, we may all come together to confront a problem or a crisis or a common enemy, but as that need dissipates, so does the coherence. The dissipation is the chaos stage.

What techniques other than threat or fear, whether real or manufactured, can bring people together with a sense of common mission? The need is to develop a climate where the individuals take the time to listen, to hear the voices of those who have different ideas and/or values, where we honestly look at our own feelings and agenda and see how there might be merger or compromise. Essential for that to happen is the presence of trust and respect. Typically, that requires time and listening and testing. It means that we open ourselves to change, to new possibilities—that we let go of our ego needs and acknowledge our vulnerability. The technique that seems most effective in moving through this stage, the emptiness stage, is a small group coming together to explore and discover themselves.

For the past few years, I have been part of such a group, made up of five couples and one widower. We are very diverse in background, age, and life experiences. We came together originally to explore and share what it meant to be a Catholic-Christian in the twenty-first century. We continue to value our diversity, but we have bonded as a family where no one is judged, where no one's ideas are rejected, and where we are a support for each other. Indeed, the four characteristics along the road to wholesome love are in evidence whenever we gather the following: forgiveness, acceptance, compassion, and then, open love. I suggest that we are a micromodel of the Church. I believe that we all feel safe and know that our secrets as well as our hopes can be discussed communally, always as an opportunity for each of us to grow in love and in holiness. I am fascinated by how revealing oneself, how opening oneself to let others see me naked rather than clothed in masks of propriety or goodness, and how with my weaknesses hidden by a fig leaf frees me to love and be loved.

This group is also an impetus toward our mission as Christ followers: to live the way of love. We are people of hope as well as of love. While we realize our responsibility to model love and joy in our daily lives, we also know that the roads to living and working to bring about the kingdom are many. Several of us are aware that our adult children do not see the Church as a potent force in their lives; some of them may not often think of the Church at all. But we rejoice as we see that they demonstrate acceptance and compassion in their lives, and I pray that my two children may have the gift of a group such as the one I described so that they can feel the joy and warmth of both freedom to be and joy in relationship. May they feel the friendship of Jesus, the God of wild love and reckless giving.

Groups, in order to survive, require some form of leadership. *The Code of Canon Law* (para. 391) spells out that the diocesan bishop "is to rule the particular church committed to him with legislative, executive and judicial power in accord with the norm of law." As I think of the group that I just described, I note that we rule the group by consensus. We do have someone who does the organizing, but all decisions are by consensus. In fact, I suspect that if we were to use the model set forth in the *Code of Canon Law* for bishops, our group would soon die. As I look at the leadership models presented in the Gospels, they seem to emphasize service rather than power. We hear Jesus speak of the shepherd and his sheep, where they know one another and where the shepherd will leave the flock to search for one stray; we hear Jesus, as he washes the feet of his disciples, describe servant leadership; and then he tells the parable of the good steward who knows that the master demands that he use the resources to increase the kingdom.

I know pastors who embody those models in Jesus's teaching; indeed, I worked for a diocesan bishop who did so. But the language of the *Code of Canon Law* seems to me to reflect a hierarchical model and style that encourages passive obedience rather than creative collaboration. The documents of Vatican II that began to erase the second-class status of the laity are not reflected in the official description of the bishop's role and power. The clerical state is not presented as a servant leadership, urging the flock to use its creative gifts to move toward holiness with the ordained and to create microcosms of the kingdom; it has the danger of placing the laity in the role of obedient servants waiting to be told what to do and how to do it.

Our participation in several communities through which we move on a daily basis opens for us the door to holiness. We can become the practitioner of the law of love, of the Jesus-message, as we interact in various settings. Our demeanor must reflect a profound sense of joy based on the awareness of God's love that is all around us, a sense of acceptance of all who hurt or live on society's margins, and a sense of compassion for those in pain. We cannot change the world, but we can help our own little world to see the joy of creation and to see that the fruits of loving are zest and freedom.

One of the roles of community is to help us see ourselves and not take ourselves too seriously. That danger seems to apply especially to leaders and, even more so, to authoritarian-style leaders. Let me close this section with a quote from Thomas Aquinas's volume *Summa contra Gentiles*: *"In human affairs whatever is against reason is a sin. Now it is against reason for anyone to be burdensome to others by offering no pleasure to them, and by hindering their enjoyment."* Amen!

Conversion

As suggested above, community provides the climate and often the stimulus for self-exploration and discovery. This process of self-exploration and self-discovery conjures up images of shortcomings and weaknesses as well as dreams of what may be possible. In other words, we may find ourselves confronted with the issue of forgiveness: Can we forgive ourselves? Can those whom we have slighted or offended in some way forgive us? Can God forgive us? Jesus has offered all of us forgiveness. There is no offense that can lie beyond the generosity of his love. To think otherwise is the height of pride, and there is no way that we can extract forgiveness from others. Either they will or they will not forgive us. The real question comes down to whether we can forgive ourselves.

Compare Francis Thompson's "The Hound of Heaven" and the passage from Thomas Wolfe cited earlier. Both are confronted with an awareness of the Jesus-message of unconditional love. Wolfe, in awe of the message, balks at its implications and turns away. Thompson, after finding that there is no hiding from the gentle but a persistent pursuer, says, "That voice is round me like a burning sea" and then concludes "O world invisible, we view thee / O world intangible, we touch thee / O world unknowable, we know thee." Thompson's poem is about conversion and is couched in the framework of God's continuing and unending offer of his love and friendship. But love and friendship demand a relationship, and relationships bring responsibilities. The final paragraph in the section above on community delineates the joy and strength that come with deep love. Yet hidden in that quote is the flip side of what happens if the love weakens and the burdens grow.

Perhaps a quick look at how the *Catechism* (para.1972) describes the new law can serve as an appropriate preface to the topic of *conversion*. It reads, "The New Law is called a *law of love* because it makes [*sic*] us act out of the love infused by the Holy Spirit, rather than from fear; a *law of grace* because it confers the strength of grace to act, by means of faith and the sacraments; a *law of freedom,* because it sets us free from the ritual and juridical observances of the Old Law, inclines us to act spontaneously by the prompting of charity and, finally, lets us pass from the condition of a servant who 'does not know what his master is doing' to that of a friend of Christ."

The love, grace, and freedom set forth in that selection from the *Catechism* is what conversion promises. Despite my very limited theological background, I do not feel comfortable with the use of the word "makes" in the first line of the quote above. Perhaps we would be more respectful of the Holy Spirit and the God-given gift of free will if we used words such as "inclines" or "moves." Conversion is a commitment to change one's life, to become a new creation, a disciple of the new law. Bernard Lonergan, the Jesuit theologian, pondered and wrote about the process of conversion. Let me confess here that I am drawing on secondary sources for this venture into Lonergan's ideas. I am not equipped to read him in the original. Lonergan presents a model of conversion that brings the person face-to-face with a number of decisions and judgments—decisions and judgments that will move the individual from an existing perspective or worldview into a radically new realm of knowing, valuing, and acting. Thus, this conversion experience has radical implications and covers three aspects of human life: intellectual conversion, moral conversion, and religious conversion.

The intellectual conversion allows the person's consciousness to move beyond the apparent reality in our world to give insight into meanings below the surface. We adopt a new way of looking at life and a new talent for integrating our experiences. The moral conversion leads us to make use of a new criterion for making judgments and decisions. The former emphasis on self and ego is replaced by an insight into the biases and prejudices inherent in our culture and our own socialization, allowing that to be replaced by the ability to judge and do what is just, compassionate, and merciful rather than what will be best for me and mine. The religious conversion is the overwhelming awareness of God's love for me and for all creation. The presence of God's love becomes the center of life for those blessed with that conversion experience.

THOMAS W. MAHAN

I know that when I think about conversion, the examples of Paul and Peter leap to mind. Paul (then known as Saul), on his way to Damascus, is stricken blind and hears God's voice asking why he is persecuting the disciples of Jesus. From this experience, Paul emerges a new man and commits his life to evangelizing the gentile world. Peter boldly claimed that he would be faithful to Jesus even to death, but three times denied knowing him when persons connected him with Jesus. Then, in seeing the look on Jesus's face, he became overwhelmed with grief and embraced a whole new commitment. Yet for me, and I suspect for most people, conversion does not come like these lightning bolts. I have been blessed with a sudden insight, maybe even an epiphany, on occasion when reading or listening to a homily or quietly meditating, which confronts me with a delicious awareness of Jesus's love and the love that is infused throughout all creation.

I am grateful for those occasional blessings, and I wonder if those gentle reminders are what we "cradle Catholics" are to expect since our baptismal initiation came before our capacity to understand what our parents and godparents were agreeing to for us. I present *conversion* as a path to holiness and to our participation in working to bring about the kingdom because for me (maybe for everybody?), this conversion is a continuing process. It is true that I am saved through the love of Jesus, but only if I choose to accept it. The acceptance is not a simple yes or no; my behaviors and my attitudes provide the yes or the no.

A friend, now deceased, who served as the abbot of the Trappist community outside of Charleston, South Carolina, Dom Francis Kline, OCSO, in his dying days completed a little volume entitled *Four Ways of Holiness for the Universal Church* (Kalamazoo, MI: Cistercian Publications, 2007). Those four ways—namely conversion, suffering, desire, and unity—have much overlap with the four themes that I am using. He writes (p. 7), "Great and sudden conversions play a part in this process of the baptismal grace, but they are no substitute for it. They must be seen as turning points, pivotal events, perhaps, that lead us to more subtle conversions as we continue to work out our salvation until the end." Abbot Kline then goes on to quote Cardinal John Henry Newman where he stated, "Growth is the only evidence of life." It is this model of conversion as an ongoing process that continues until the death of our bodies that is a road to holiness.

When, as a seminarian in my undergraduate studies, I read Bernanos's novel, the *Diary of a Country Priest,* my eyes were opened to the wonderful mercy and love of God. The priest-protagonist in the novel whose life has been belittled and disparaged by most, including prominent parishioners, priest colleagues, and his superiors, is dying and goes to visit a classmate who has left the priesthood and is living with a woman. The lapsed priest tries to hide his mistress's existence and to cover his leaving the priesthood with intellectual reasons. During the night, our hero collapses and briefly regains consciousness and asks the friend to give him absolution. Reluctantly, the friend accedes but is troubled. Then come the words that have haunted me through the past sixty-plus years: *Does it matter? Grace is everywhere.* I try to keep those words before me as my remembrance that there is no basis for my allowing feelings of misery or of sadness or of anger or of hurt or of pain to cloud my conviction of God's unconditional love. For me, that is the source of growth in forgiveness, in acceptance of diversity and differentness, in compassion for all humanity and each person with whom I have contact, and in my efforts to cleanse my love of self-interest, judgment, and ego. Those efforts demand daily renewal, but the grace that is everywhere keeps those efforts alive.

Cross

I probably should have titled this section "Suffering" since that is essentially what I wish to look at. Still, Jesus's words were this: *"Whoever wishes to come after me must deny himself, take up his **cross**, and follow me . . . For the son of man will come with his angels in his Father's glory, and then he will repay all according to his conduct"* (Matthew 16). Richard Rohr, the prolific Franciscan priest writes of "great love" and "great suffering" as doors to transformation. Both of those experiences can awaken us to the awareness and acceptance of our vulnerability and encourage us to become more open, more willing to surrender our ego controls (*The Naked Now*, New York: Crossroad Publishing, 2009). Abbot Kline who died a very extended and painful death describes that awareness in his book *Four Ways of Holiness*. Here are his words written about eight months before his death:

The question of who is our neighbor becomes moot. All are our neighbors. Everyone. Barriers fall, prejudices shrink, opportunities appear when we love the neighbor and offer love when he is temporarily out of his wits, or when she has for the moment forgotten her dignity. Love insists on the noble, sees through to the essential, ignores the ugly, intuits the beautiful, deflects the violence from its own destructive blindness and waits for its redirection for the good. (op. cit., p. 7)

Lord, help me to live that love!

However, most of us hope and pray that we can be spared the experience of Abbot Francis, that we will not be afflicted with an extended, disabling, extremely painful assault on our physical being. Yet most lives cannot escape the pain of loss or disappointment and cannot avoid the feeling of aloneness or of being misunderstood. These facts bring us back to the idea of original sin and the allegory of Adam and Eve in the Garden of Eden. As I mentioned earlier, I believe that the allegory is just that. It is a story without any historical base, but one that does teach a basic, important message. The message is that we humans are what Nietzsche called the incarnation of dissonance. Basic to our being is the search for God, the restlessness with all the pleasures and goods of the world because they do not fulfill us, do not make us feel complete. At the same time, our being also desires and takes pleasure in these aspects of the created world. It is easy for us to become addicted to or trapped by those desires and forget that true joy and happiness can be found only by embracing the love that gave us life, the love that is God. So our desires and natural appetites lead us to create new gods and abandon the God who created and loves us. Free will is at the essence of original sin.

Earlier in this volume, I admitted that I do not have an explanation for all the disasters, catastrophes, epidemics, and the like that have confronted us through recorded history. I find it very difficult to endorse the concepts of ransoming us from our sinful ways or that only through the passion and death of Jesus could humankind be saved. Rather, I am inclined to adopt a view that sees creation as in process, as incomplete, but that all creation is moving toward completion through the presence of grace. Indeed, we see that, even with the atrocities that have assaulted people in this and the twentieth centuries, there is a growing thrust toward compassion, toward acceptance of others, and toward awareness of the unity of all humanity. This perspective, which owes much to Pierre Teilhard de Chardin, SJ, brings with it faith that any diminishment of each of us emerges from the incompleteness of nature, the cosmic evolutionary process. I believe that God supports our efforts to get free of diminishment, to resist it but without bitterness, resentment, or revolt. These diminishments, whether personal or communal or widespread, are part of the evolutionary process, which brings with it conflicts, competition, loss, failure, and the like. At the same time, evolution brings about greater complexity, which, in turn, leads to new perspectives, new challenges, and change.

So then how does the *cross* or suffering open for us the door to holiness. I would suggest that our hurts and pains, our losses and disappointments, and our confusions and our doubts—all can be spurs to work to reduce such experiences for others as well as ourselves by embracing and expressing our Jesus-based love through forgiveness, acceptance, compassion, and love. In addition, we can also, even if in a very minor fashion, feel empathy for Jesus who loved us and died to teach us the importance of love if we are to be his followers. I recall on the night of my late wife's sudden death, when all I had been feeling was numbness, doubt, and confusion, and somehow I found myself in the backyard, naked in a drenching downpour, when the thought flashed in my mind of how grateful I was for the thirty-five years of wonder and wow that had been mine. That image and that thought are as vivid today as they were on 25 February 2004. Grace really is everywhere!

Nonviolence, Forgiveness, Compassion

I suspect that few people would disagree with the statement that we live in a violent world. In fact, it is clear that the Catholic Church, my church which I love, has been active over many centuries in doing violence. Yet the message of the Gospels, as I read them, is consistently a message of nonviolence from Jesus. Still, the *Catechism of the Catholic Church, Second Edition,* has no listing of nonviolence in its index or its glossary. The treatment in the *Catechism of Catholic Church* of the fifth commandment (para 2258-2330), "Thou shalt not kill," skirts the issue of Jesus's teaching of nonviolence even though (para. 2262) the authors point out that Jesus, in the Sermon on the Mount, adds a proscription of anger, hatred, and vengeance to the meaning of the commandment. My favorite resource for issues spiritual and/or theological, Thomas Aquinas, seems not to have dealt with the topic of nonviolence though I do not know just what the comparable Latin term would be. I do note, however, that, in his discussion of courage and fortitude, Thomas writes, "The principal act of fortitude is endurance, that is, to stand immovable in the midst of dangers rather than to attack them," and also "Endurance is more difficult than aggression." That sounds like an endorsement of the principle of nonviolence. So how central to Jesus's message is the practice of nonviolence? I believe that it is at the heart of his human life's message—the heart of his constant emphasis on love as the path to God who is love.

I am aware that there are paradoxes. Some might prefer to call them contradictions in the portrayal of Jesus in the four canonical Gospels. Nonetheless, I feel that his emphasis on forgiveness, his constant call through his actions for compassion and acceptance even of the sinners especially rejected by the Jewish people—tax collectors and prostitutes—along with his frequent rejection of violence even in the face of personal abuse and death leave little doubt about Jesus's teaching that his way is the way of nonviolence. It is a difficult standard that once again touts openness and acceptance of vulnerability rather than defensiveness and aggressive response.

For me, it is difficult to imagine a concept of holiness that does not have nonviolence as a prominent component. Violence along with its somewhat more subtle cousins—anger, prejudice, hatred, and slander—is in direct opposition to the second of Jesus's two commandments: to love others as we love ourselves. The beatitudes as set forth in the Gospels of both Matthew and Luke take us further down the path of holiness where we are challenged not only to respond with caring and concern with the world's social ills but also to lay aside temptations to judge and condemn while forgiving and accepting. We are reminded in Matthew's final beatitude that we may well be isolated and rejected for putting aside violence and its cousins. Instead, we should rejoice and be glad for we have chosen to be true disciples of the Jesus-message.

I have to confess, as I write this section on these four paths to holiness, which seem to me so intimately connected to Vatican II's universal call to holiness, I wonder at my church's apparent downplay of community, conversion, cross, and nonviolence. Perhaps I should acknowledge that the cross does get some significant emphasis, but in my view, it is twisted. The cross, rather than being a symbol to evoke awe over the love and generosity of God in the person of Jesus, is presented as the vehicle that rescues humanity from "this valley of tears." We are not, in my eyes, "the poor banished children of Eve." We are the loved creatures of the God of wild love and reckless giving who has placed us on this planet to use this creation to do good, to live in joy, and to discover holiness through loving the Creator-Teacher-Lover-Sanctifier and through loving all humanity. The words of St. Teresa of Avila spring to mind: "From silly devotions and sour-faced saints, O Lord, deliver us."

Thomas Aquinas tells us that "wonder is the beginning of learning. It causes delight because it carries with it the hope of discovery." My wonder is what would happen if my church were to place a moratorium on such activities as talk about individual sin and "protecting society from evil" legislation like the recognition of same-sex marriage and on encouraging vocal, frightening demonstrations against abortion and instead proclaim without ceasing that we are the people of God, the people committed to showing love (read "Forgiveness, Acceptance, Compassion") to all people in all situations, the people who recognize that grace is everywhere, but know that Jesus taught us what the cost of such love can be. Imagine what could happen if in every archdiocesan and diocesan in the United States, the archbishop/bishop would host a monthly celebration of God as love with the entire community invited. The celebration could close with the invitation to all who believe in the God of love to share in the Eucharist and with the charge to go forth to practice forgiveness, acceptance, compassion, and even passionate love each day until we come together the next month. What an experiment that would be!

THE JOY OF CATHOLICISM!

IN THE SPRING of 1964, I was riding with a colleague from the Connecticut State Department of Education on Interstate 91 toward New Haven when out of the blue, he asked, "Tom, why do you continue to stay a Catholic?" The query came from a gentleman whom I had known for ten years, and he, with his French Canadian background, had been raised a Catholic. But as an adult, he had first been a lapsed Catholic and then had joined the Congregational Church. I was amazed at the words that came immediately from my mouth. "Because it is a religion of joy, and I don't know any other religion where joy is the main theme" was my response. I could have mentioned the wonderful emphasis on redemption, the constant message of forgiveness, and the implications of Jesus's incarnation to the meaning of being human, but I came up with joy. It is the answer that continues to resound in my heart and in my mind.

Love and joy are an inseparable pair. Aquinas writes, "The only person who truly has joy is one who lives in love." In both my own experience and my observations of others, that statement is confirmed. St. Thomas even goes further when he tell us that "it is appropriate to say that love and joy are the only two human emotions that we can attribute literally to God." To me, that means that loving and feeling joy-filled are ways that we imitate God in whose image we are created. The Catholic Church has proclaimed this God of love and joy and this God who so loves humanity that Jesus came to teach us how to love and find joy by his example. What is more attractive in human life than love? We all pursue it, either in relationships or in possessions, but it brings joy only in relationships. Indeed, the joy that comes from loving needs to be shared. We note on the faces and on the behaviors of persons in love a warmth, a sense of wholeness that were not there previously. I believe that God's joy overflows with such force that it calls us, attracts us until we either search for that presence or we embrace substitute after substitute in its stead.

I feel sorry for those people who, as they look at the world in which we live, see only pain, suffering, hunger, violence, and oppression. There is no question that those are curses that haunt life here on earth, yet even in those communities ravaged by such trials, we find people experiencing moments of joy and showing care and love for their neighbors. Children still play, parents and children still show affection and care for each other, and complete strangers are often seen sharing and/or caring for someone more deeply in need. The human capacity for affection, for empathy, and for the quest for joy is found in the midst of squalor as well as in the midst of plenty. Love is critical to human development, and the comment that the novelist Bernanos puts in the mouth of the country priest as he speaks to the countess in the chateau presents the other side of that fact: "Hell, madam, is never to love again."

If joy is a by-product of love and God is love, then a true religion must also be committed to proclaiming love and joy. At the center of my church's belief and practice is that proclamation (even if sometimes obscured by other actions and events). As both the *Catechism* (para. 1324) and the Vatican II *Dogmatic Constitution on the Church (Lumen Gentium)* in number 11 state, the Eucharist "is the summit and source" of our spiritual life. The Eucharist is the presence of Jesus, the embodiment of God's love, inviting us to come feast with him. This communion of believers with God is the heart of the Mass, which is, as I have said earlier, itself a *dialogue of love* between God and his people. God invites us unconditionally into the warmth of forgiveness, acceptance, compassion, and love. At the same time, he presents us with opportunities to share and spread this love, to reach out with our own acts of forgiveness, acceptance, compassion, and love. Love is contagious; it cries out to be shared.

The Church tells us that the entire universe is infused with God's love. *Grace is everywhere.* These few lines from the Jesuit poet Gerard Manley Hopkins makes that point beautifully: *"For Christ plays in ten thousand places, / Lovely in limbs and lovely in eyes not his, / To the Father through the features of men's faces."* The fact that the Church teaches that there are seven sacraments can easily distract us from the fact that all creation is sacramental. The Church recognizes seven very special opportunities in which the people of God celebrate, as a community, the gift of God's love to those receiving the sacrament. These seven differ in many respects. For example, some (baptism and confirmation) can be received only once and leave an indelible mark. Some are such that people are encouraged to receive them as often as possible (Eucharist and reconciliation). Others are restricted by conditions. Marriage can be repeated if a spouse has died. Holy orders has three levels—deacon, priest, bishop. Anointing of the sick can be "repeated whenever the sick person again falls into a serious sickness . . . or whenever a more serious crisis develops during the same sickness" (*Code of Canon Law* para. 1004, sec. 2).

Earlier in this chapter, I used the term "sacramental," which also has a technical meaning within the Church that varies some from my use. The official sacramentals are blessings for specific purposes and include not only prayers but also such actions as receiving the ashes on Ash Wednesday, the distribution of palms on Passion Sunday, and even exorcisms. While these official sacramentals usually require "a cleric who has been given the necessary power" (*Code of Canon Law*, para. 1168) as minister, "some can be administered by laypersons who are endowed with the appropriate qualities" (ibid.).

Yet in truth, all creation is sacramental in that it is an outward sign of God's love that can lead us to awe or thanksgiving or praise: sunrises and sunsets, the wildness of the ocean, the wonder at the intricacy of a spider's web, the beauty of flowers, and the taste of chocolate or wine or filet mignon. All these, and remember the lines from Hopkins above about Christ playing in all our faces are occasions of grace that is the free, unconditional gift of God's love available to everybody. No special ministers or clergy are required. The grace is there for our taking. What other word than "joy" can be used to describe a religion, a spiritual way based on such of an image? Moral theologians have written about occasions of sin, but the world is filled with the occasions of grace. Indeed, those same worldly objects and images that can distract us from God can be even more potent as doors to God. Two more quotations from Thomas Aquinas underline these thoughts: "Creatures of themselves do not withdraw us from God, but lead us to God" and "The perfect activity of a conscious being is invariably pleasurable activity. Delight is connatural to human nature."

Just as fear is at the root of despair, so hope is at the root of daring. I like to describe Jesus, God present in our flesh and world, as the God of wild love and reckless giving. Equally important to me is another facet of God that was planted in my consciousness in embryo form during my preteen years. During the years when I was in grades five through eight, I lived in a small city in eastern Connecticut. It was a struggling community that had been a mill town with a population largely descended from French Canadian stock. In fact, the sermons in the only Catholic Church in this city were all in French except that after the nine o'clock Mass, one could stay for a second sermon in Polish. The school attached to the parish was operated by the Daughters of the Holy Ghost (now, no doubt, the Daughters of the Holy Spirit), a French order who also ran the religious education program on Saturday mornings for those of us who attended the public schools.

It was in that setting that I was brought to see the Holy Spirit as God's presence throughout creation, sanctifying and strengthening us humans. Prior to that, the Holy Ghost/Spirit was just the third name in the sign of the cross, the third person in the triune God. It is not that I had any clear idea of what those words meant, but when the nun teaching my class gave me a medal in the form of a dove of the Holy Spirit, I wore it proudly on a chain around my neck. I began to turn to this Holy Spirit as the person or aspect of God close to me, touching my flesh—the person to whom I could whisper my worries or concerns or needs. That continuing experience introduced me to God as a person with whom I could talk and on whom I could depend. When, some five years later as a minor seminarian, I read Bernanos's the *Diary of a Country Priest* and was struck by the words "grace is everywhere," my spiritual life took on a new intensity. I knew that the Holy Spirit was everywhere. What a joy!

As I write these words, I am aware of how fortunate, how blessed I am to have these beliefs, this faith. Is what I believe really true? Is Jesus really the God of wild love and reckless giving? Is all creation saturated with God's presence? Is everybody and everything an occasion of grace? I am aware that I cannot offer any proofs for these beliefs, yet I am confident of their truth. Does that mean that I have no doubts? No. I do have some doubts that come and go. I know no more than anyone else what happens after the death of my physical body. I feel comfortable with the expectation that there is a life after death; after all, that has been a tenet of religious belief for many cultures and peoples throughout known history. It seems to be an intrinsic quality of human life, but it is no proof. I also have no proof about many things in this world, but deep in my heart, I believe in them. I believe that I will love and care for and be faithful to my wife so long as I have life. I have no doubt about that, but I can give no guarantee. The fact that I was able to experience that love and fidelity with my late wife gives me added assurance that I will do the same again, but I cannot guarantee what will happen or even what I will do in the future.

In a very real sense, my beliefs and my joy are built on hope. I have titled this little volume, *Faith Burning with Hope*, and with Kierkegaard, I see faith as a leap, and with Aquinas, I see hope as the father of daring. I know that some spiritual writers see hope as a danger, as an illusion that can bring suffering and disappointment. But I see hope as one of humanity's great gifts—the gift that makes us aware of possibilities and allows us to dream. Without the courage to dream, which is always hope based, life is reduced to passive detachment or frenzied pursuit of stimulants, some very worthwhile, but both of those strategies are essentially distractions from exploring and discovering the resources hidden deep in our psyches—the resources that call us to forgiveness, acceptance, and compassion, which are the doors to love of God, others, and self.

I think of a brilliant man whom I much admired who is now dead. He was an internationally known psychologist who befriended me and gave me much guidance as well as encouragement. He was a tireless worker in the areas of social justice and antipoverty programs. As old age forced him into retirement, he became bitter and close to despair. I commented to him that he had given up on his ideals with the attitude that, since he had failed to change the world, the world could not be changed. He did not like that interpretation at the time, but he lived to thank me for that insight. The point of that example, however, is to draw attention to the fullness of the Jesus-message. Jesus calls us to the way of love, and he provides the nourishment to sustain those commitments. Yet Jesus's life makes very clear that living his example leads to the probability of rejection, humiliation, and suffering. Indeed, he says in the Sermon on the Mount (Matthew 5-7), "Blessed are you when they insult you and persecute you and utter every kind of evil against you because of me." In other words, we cannot expect that our eager embrace of the way of love will change the world, but it will change *us* if we *give* our love. The joy of giving, of seeing Christ light up in the eyes of the oppressed and downtrodden comes from our empathy, our being with them even if this glimmer lasts but seconds. Many are the cases that proclaim this wise comment from Aquinas: "When anyone loves someone, whatever they suffer for their friend does not burden them; whence love makes all burdensome and impossible things light."

Love and joy are intimately connected with empathy which again is tied to our ability to forgive. Where these facts become especially relevant is in regard to our love of self. I doubt that we can become followers of the Jesus-message of love until we can see ourselves honestly, look at our secrets and hidden memories/feelings, and accept them. The sacrament of reconciliation, if used for this exploration and discovery of self followed by the expression/discussion of the discoveries, is truly a source of joy so long as we accept God's undiminished love for us. One of the keys to joy is our willingness to acknowledge and live with our human vulnerability. Joy seems to arise in the midst of humble awareness of the gift of life and our opportunities to give and share.

I know that some readers will feel that my description of Catholicism as a spiritual journey of joy is Pollyanna-ish. Yet I see it as profoundly realistic.

The challenge is to shift our mind-set about the essential meaning of the life of Jesus. I would suggest that the incarnation is the central symbol of that message, and the crucifixion is the final demonstration/proof of that message. And the message is very simple: Jesus has come out of unbelievable love to teach us how to live—that is, how to love. There is no glossing over the tribulations of human existence. Jesus, in fact, is for me a paradox, the living integration of what the poet John Keats saw as exact opposites, the poet who gives balm to hurts and the dreamer who vexes our spirits with what could be. Jesus is the embodiment of the two, which are now two sides of love: the consoler and healer and at the same time the voice that calls us to be more than we are by sharing who we are and what we have without reservation.

In closing this section, I want to restate that the joy of Catholicism is not a private, personal joy. The Church is, or perhaps more honestly, struggling to become a community of rejoicing and joy. But we need to face an important spiritual and psychological fact: joy is a choice. It is, of course, also a gift, but the gift is available to all. Neither temperament nor events nor situations can rob us of joy though such factors may cause some temporary sense of loss or separation. As I mentioned earlier, when my wife, Aline, died suddenly, I felt cut off from joy and numb to physical sensations. Suddenly, I was reminded of the thirty-five years of love and caring that I had experienced with her, and joy burst through, overwhelming the sadness and restoring my aliveness to God's presence, to the fact that grace is everywhere. There are those in the Church who fear joy because joy is free and passionate. With the focus on love and compassion, the joyful may often forget or ignore man-made rules and regulations. That will certainly be upsetting to those who have chosen fear over love, caution over joy. When the focus is on the Vatican II emphasis on the "universal call to holiness," we are, in my mind, concerned with how to help all believers become passionate lovers. When Jesus, according to the final words of Matthew's Gospel (28 and 20), tells the disciples to go forth to all nations "teaching them to observe all that I commanded you," what else could be the center of that teaching than his law of love? And love is the father of joy, the conqueror of fear.

THE CHURCH FACES THE TWENTY-FIRST CENTURY

T HE DOCUMENTS OF Vatican II would seem to have been designed to prepare the Catholic Church for being a leadership force in this century where the dignity of the human person is front and center across issues and geography. Sadly, much of the vision of those documents has been relegated to bookshelves or has been reinterpreted to support traditional practices and positions. It seems to me that the Church, despite Blessed Pope John XXIII's encouragement of openness and interaction with the world, has taken a defensive and reactionary stance. Certainly, there are trends in today's world that pose serious challenges and, in some instances, threats to established practices and policies that are rooted in the Jesus-message and the example of his life. But even there, how we interact is important. If we do not listen to others, we have no reason to expect that they will listen to us. I want to portray how, in my mind, some of the current issues that create potential conflicts with traditional Church practice might be incorporated positively into Church teaching and action. These thoughts are based on the optimism of Thomas Aquinas whose approach to the Christian life could be summarized by "what can I do to achieve happiness or delight?" rather than on the post-Tridentine "what does the law require?" In other words, I want to return to an approach that is focused on a joyful goal and reject the approach of "how do I avoid punishment?" (See Bouchard, *Theological Studies 63*, 2002, pp. 539-558.)

The Church and the Existence of Evil

I suspect that few people would doubt that evil exists, but what does that mean if we believe that all creation is the work of a loving God who brought things into being as good? The *Catechism* (para. 401) specifically rejects the idea that there is a rival being (Satan or the devil) who is warring with God for domination. Still, that same *Catechism* describes renegade spiritual beings (angels) who, given the free will, have chosen to rebel and have become seducers of humanity. In fact, in the introduction of John's Gospel, we read of Jesus being "the light of the world" and the darkness did not overcome it. Something in my mind has trouble with this image of a powerful, dark force contesting God's grace and love for the control of us humans.

Thomas Aquinas, for me, solves this dilemma when he tells us that evil is not "something"; it is the lack of something, the lack of good. Earlier in this manuscript, I referred to a quote from the *Nuremberg Diary* where the author, G. M. Gilbert, comes to the conclusion from his experience with the war crimes trials that "evil . . . is the absence of empathy." For me, that makes Aquinas's definition take on concrete reality. I am not sure that we need, except as mythological beings similar in kind to Adam and Eve, Satan or the devil or Lucifer. Our free will and the fact that we are a composite, designed by God, of flesh and spirit is adequate basis for explaining how we can (and do) seek pleasure and delight in actions and objects that obscure our connection to the divine, to our purpose. If we can adopt this approach to evil, perhaps we can eliminate some of those prayers, which to me seem abhorrent for a God of love. How do we justify, in light of the Jesus-message, prayers that ask God "to cast into hell Satan and the other evil spirits" or that picture us as "the banished children of Eve, mourning and weeping in this vale of tears" or caution us about "the devil, who like a raging lion, goes about seeking whom he may devour"? If there should be spiritual beings who, like us humans, have lost their sense of connection to the Creator, why are they excluded from the saving power of Jesus and the Holy Spirit?

If we are to base our moral theology on God's goodness and on the fact that we are daily encompassed by occasions of grace, and if we see in the lack of the development of empathy the source of our sinfulness, then we need to rethink our approach to faith development, especially for our youth and adults. If we look at the six commandments that fall under the "thou shalt not . . ." umbrella, we find that each of them has to do with failing to respect the dignity of others, with placing ourselves first no matter who may be injured. The same is true if we analyze the five sins, which I described in the chapter "Sanctity, Sex, and Sin" as the pivotal sins for our era—anger, deceit, fear, greed, and pride—all tear at our connection to each other and thus to God. The question that seems central for bishops, pastors, and religious educators is, how do we develop empathy in our people?

I have intentionally avoided the word "teach" since much teaching in the catechetical world has followed the gas station model—fill them up, just pour the facts in. Yet the very word "educate" means to draw forth, and Aquinas tells us that wonder or amazement is the beginning of learning. How can we go about helping our faithful become more skilled at empathy, at the forgiveness that should flow from empathy, and at the compassion that cannot exist without both empathy and forgiveness? Our friend Thomas Aquinas tells us that it is in showing compassion that we most clearly imitate God.

I realize that many authors and publishers of catechetical materials have much improved the instructional materials to bring the faith alive for all ages. Our goal in our faith communities is needed to create *enthusiasm for the faith,* and the heart of that faith is the embrace of the way of love and the celebration of the Eucharist as the continuous renewal of the gift of that love. For me, that goal clearly suggests that our instructional efforts need to be aimed as much at the emotional life of our faithful as at their cognitive awareness of Church teaching and the Gospels. We need to build a curriculum that is highly experiential, involves simulations and case studies, and calls for self-awareness as well as openness to other perspectives. We all need to find ourselves deeply immersed in what it means to forgive even when we hurt, what it means to have compassion and care for someone even when we are at risk or uncomfortable, and what it means to love unconditionally even when we are rejected or betrayed. Films, novels, dramatic reenactments can help this process of exploring, discovering, and then living what it means to answer Jesus's invitation to follow him.

The teaching function of the Church should be built on our relationships, focus on the affective side of life, open us to models for change, encourage prayer and self-awareness as well as self-disclosure, allow for vulnerability in a setting of care and support, and lead to avenues for conversion and commitment. The Vatican's *General Directory for Catechesis* (Washington, DC, 1998, para. 85-86) sets forth six fundamental tasks for the development of disciples that can be summarized as follows: education for community life, moral development, missionary initiative, teaching to pray, liturgical education, and knowledge of the faith. The first three listed above demand, in my mind, the approach that I have been trying to describe and that I summarized in the first sentence of this paragraph. The last three in the list provide nourishment for the personal embrace of the Jesus-message.

The Church and the Challenge of Leadership

The *Code of Canon Law* (para. 386-391) and *The Catechism of the Catholic Church* (para. 888-896) both spell out a triad of functions for bishops: teaching, sanctifying, and leading (the cited documents use the term "governing" rather than "leading," but since they also use the image of the good shepherd, I have chosen to see the bishop as a leader). As an introduction to my thoughts about the questionable effectiveness of the traditional perception of a bishop's role of leader that seems to me similar to the "divine right of kings" model, I want to refer to the paper that the Jesuit John O'Malley wrote to commemorate the fortieth anniversary of the opening of Vatican II. O'Malley sees the council as reflecting a dramatic change in the how of Church operations, which he summarizes in five areas: from a heavily vertical behavioral style to one of cooperation, collaboration, and collegiality; from a control mentality to a serving mentality; from a static, look-to-the-past perspective to an openness to the evolution of concepts and a focus on the future; from a vocabulary of exclusion (excommunication and anathema) to a philosophy of inclusion; and from a climate of lay passive acceptance to active participation and engagement by all the people of God. Father O'Malley expands his ideas in his book, *What Happened at Vatican II (Cambridge, MA: Harvard University Press, 2010).*

I could not imagine a healthier model of leadership for interacting with the climate of the twenty-first century than the one which O'Malley discerned in the operations of Vatican II, yet somehow, this style, prominent in the council actions and decrees, appears to have been zealously ignored by the Vatican and by many bishops around the world. There are exceptions, of course, and I had the pleasure of working with such an exceptional bishop-*leader* who realized that if you want to have followers, you need to listen. For three years, David B. Thompson, DD, JCL, now the retired bishop of Charleston, went about the state of South Carolina listening to his priests and his people. At the end of that time, he convened the Synod of Charleston with his pastoral letter entitled "Our Heritage—Our Hope" that introduced a three-year process that involved wide participation from every parish, mission, and religious community in the diocese. This is not the place to describe in detail the synod's process that rose from the many faith communities throughout the diocese to the twelve study area committees to the plenary sessions where every faith community had a representative. But it is relevant to point out how a bishop in a

THOMAS W. MAHAN

geographically large area where Catholics make up a small percentage of the population could clearly embody the five style changes that O'Malley describes. The titles that Bishop Thompson used for his documents in this process communicate his pastoral, caring vision. His pastoral letter to close the synod and announce the structure for the implementation of its recommendations was titled "Souvenir and Promise" while his document to present the actual implementation design bore the title "Enthusiasm for the Faith."

I mentioned how Bishop Thompson led the Synod of Charleston and promulgated its recommendations and conclusions as simply an example of his style. That same style characterized his entire episcopate, which included the ease with which he gave credit to others for achievements which owed much to him. I know that there are other bishops who also operated with a listening ear, an open mind, and a caring heart, but I, like many others, am painfully aware of some who prize their authoritarian style that seems to be supported by the *Code of Canon Law* (para. 381, sec. 1-2). I am not advocating a democratic model. I am simply suggesting that the council's emphasis on the dignity of the person demands that diocesan as well as universal Church leadership listen, be open to new approaches and interpretations, and recognize the human fallibility that is characteristic even of the Supreme Pontiff who might better be viewed as the vicar of Christ in the roles of the great bridge-builder (*pontifex maximus*) and the servant of the servants of God (*servus servorum Dei*).

In light of the emphasis on the three major functions of a bishop—teaching, sanctifying, and ruling or governing *(Code,* para. 375 and *Catechism,* para. 888 and 893-894), does anyone else wonder why the academic areas where those selected to be bishops are to hold either a doctorate degree, or at least the licentiate, are specifically named *(Code,* para. 378) as "sacred scripture, theology, or canon law" where expertise in the functions of teaching and leading (ruling/governing) are ignored? There is no mention about academic background in psychology or pedagogy or human relations or organizational behavior/development as even desirable in either the *Catechism* or the *Code* even though the effectiveness of a bishop is heavily dependent on understandings, insights, and skills in those areas. Leadership requires vision combined with sensitivity to the needs of those served, the willingness and capacity to listen, the creativity to integrate diverse perspectives into a synthesis, and the courage to admit when one has been wrong. Blessed Pope John XXIII, Joseph Cardinal Bernardin, Archbishop Rembert Weakland, and Bishops David Thompson and Kenneth Untener have all been exemplars of that model, but I fear that they are not only exceptions, but that they may be among the last of a dying breed.

The Church and the Secular World: Collaborators or Enemies?

Even the persons on the street whose attention to world affairs have been limited find themselves impacted by what is happening in the governments, in the financial centers, and in the battlegrounds in the fight to control terrorism. It is obvious that most of what determines policies and actions in those critical areas emerges from a culture of fear. I do not question that these actions are appropriate though I do question some of the tactics associated with them. However, such policies and actions will not create peace. We know from history that violence creates violence. We know that fear brings with it tendencies toward deceit and distrust. The United Nations, intended to be an arbiter for justice across nations, finds itself having to rely on sanctions and verbal condemnations, which again fail to be vehicles for peace.

In my youth, if my memory is still working with some accuracy, our emphasis was that we were a pilgrim church, a church that warned the faithful about the dangers of the world and the temptations in that world that could lead us to eternal damnation. Vatican II, with the promulgation of the *Pastoral Constitution on the Church in the Modern World (Gaudium et Spes)* on 8 December 1965 by Pope Paul VI endorsed a diametrically opposed vision. The council fathers, the bishops from around the world, approved the document with a vote of 2,309-75 on 7 December, announcing the Church's embrace of the world as God's gift to humanity, as the Church's challenge to offer to all humanity how we can join and work with the Holy Spirit in the movement of the world toward its destiny. With 97 percent of the council fathers endorsing the platform, the *Pastoral Constitution on the Church in the Modern World* pictures the Church and the human society as partners in bringing about the kingdom. The image of the world as a "vale of tears" through which we must pass in hurt and sadness is changed to the challenge where the followers of Jesus have to interact through faith with the world. In the words of the said constitution (para. 38), "The fundamental law of human perfection, and consequently the transformation of the world, is the new commandment of love. He [Jesus] assures those who trust in the charity of God that the way of love is open to all men [*sic*] and that the effort to establish a universal brotherhood will not be in vain."

Earlier in the document, the council fathers underline the role of dialogue, of working with those who differ from the Church, toward the benefit of humanity. At the heart of that emphasis are the statements on the dignity of the person and the need to eradicate all signs and actions that lead to discrimination against individuals or groups. The authors of the document state boldly the call to love and respect our enemies (para. 34) and remind us that "God alone is the judge and searcher of hearts: he forbids us to pass judgment on the inner guilt of others. The teaching of Christ even demands that we forgive injury, and the precept of love, which is the commandment of the New Law, includes all our enemies."

The enemy of the Church is not the world; it is the culture of fear, which, I sense, has infected the Church as well. Each of us, as individuals and as groups or organizations, is confronted with a choice: do we choose love, hope, and openness or do we choose fear, deceit, and despair. There is no middle ground unless you consider escapism as a choice. But that—whether it takes the form of pleasure, work, alcohol/drugs, or do-goodism—is the coward's cover for choosing fear, deceit, and despair even though it may be done with a smile painted on our faces. It is not, of course, a one-time choice. Situations and events confront us time and again with the choice. Love and fear cannot coexist; the great discovery, in the words of Aquinas, is that joy is the product of love and that "zeal arises from the intensity of love."

I wonder if we have misdesigned our catechetical programs for youth, young adults, and adults. The essence of the Christian faith is found in each individual's personal relationship with Jesus, and that relationship is based on the fact that he is love incarnate—our lover who showed us the joy and the price of love. Central to that relationship is the belief that his loving presence is especially with us in the Eucharist but is also with us throughout creation. Our bodies are the most precious instrument for awareness of that presence, and our interactions with others provide us with the wonder-filled opportunity to see Jesus in every other person. This is especially intriguing since that same Jesus loves every person, and we believers love him. Thus, we have the roots of a unique community of brothers and sisters—all children of God. Our catechetical programs need to begin with sharing the awareness of that loving presence, of the call to share in the love and joy that are the divine life. How freeing that is. I remember, early in my seminary career, when I was struck by the immensity of God's love, both in the events and sayings of Jesus's life and also in the wonders of our human emotions and the delights of our body. The awareness that grace is everywhere, that everything I think or do can be an occasion of grace is remarkably freeing. Many of my friends have commented that they see (and even felt) religion as tying them down, as taking away freedom, as imposing rules and regulations. I have tried to share the tremendous sense of freedom, of openness, of daring that has been my experience from my Catholic faith. Dogma and doctrine come into being as we seek to grasp the nature of the divine, as we try to understand, always unsuccessfully, who God is and the why of his creation. Those efforts, while drawn from scripture and tradition, are the work of humans struggling to help us grasp the ungraspable.

In the end, catechesis must be rooted in love of God and of neighbor (including our enemies). The process of developing and growing in faith must begin with an awareness of love and move from there to exploring one's own experiences, feelings, and needs in a supportive environment. Is there a sense of resonance with Augustine's "restless heart"? Are there examples of sudden gifts of grace? When do you find your joy? That process of discovery then leads to both the expression of what one has found and, we pray, to the wish to make the leap that can free us from the chains of our fears, our hurts, and our anxieties. We accept our profound desires, make the *choice* to believe, and see those desires fulfilled only by becoming a passionate lover.

THOMAS W. MAHAN

ENTHUSIASM FOR THE FAITH

I DEBATED WHETHER TO title this chapter as I have above or as "Joy and Hope," the English translation of the first three Latin words of the *Pastoral Constitution on the Church in the Modern World.* In a sense, both considered titles convey much the same message, but I chose the title that Bishop Thompson had used for the publication of his design for implementing the Synod of Charleston. "Enthusiasm" comes from the Greek and means "filled with God" while the English definition carries the ideas of zest and energy. Without those qualities, faith is dead.

There may be many who will ask, How can faith bring with it zest and energy given today's world? We look about, and we see turmoil bursting into warfare in many parts of the world; starvation ravages Africa, and here, in our country, hunger and homelessness have reached shameful levels. In the United States, we see turmoil and anger and even hate as our economy collapses, as our federal government is paralyzed and dysfunctional; our state legislatures, afraid of embracing hope—steal rights from the workers and money from the schools in an attempt to placate greedy ideologues. Church leaders seem almost silent about these vicious threats to the Jesus-message and content themselves with rallies like Eucharistic congresses and with trying to influence lawmakers on issues such as outlawing abortion and rescuing marriage from what they claim is the danger inherent in same-sex unions. The picture that emerges is gloomy, if not dire.

Given those facts, how can I write about hope and joy and enthusiasm? Am I afflicted with a form of dementia where I cannot understand the magnitude of the problems, the threats, and the tragedies that are endemic in twenty-first-century society? The culture of fear is reaping the results that are inevitable when anger, deceit, greed, and pride become viewed as virtues and forgiveness, acceptance, compassion, and love are treated as impractical notions. However, let's look a little deeper. Throughout the planet, there is evidence of a greater consciousness, of awareness of the oneness of humanity, and of our need for interdependence across nations, cultures, and religions. Compassion breaks out in vivid form as the news of disasters come across the communications media. The examples of heroic service to others are found in almost every village and community. Much of the warfare has at its roots on the quest for the dignity of human life, and hope exists that the violence will rapidly be replaced with reconciliation and embrace. As a further piece of supportive evidence, we know that food production and distribution could feed the world. We are aware that we have the resources to reduce the onslaught of disease in areas of poverty. Basic needs such as water, housing, wellness, and education are in short supply only because we do not have the courage to bring them to the needy.

In other words, there are very clear signs of what seems to me to be a cosmic evolution that can become the force toward bringing about the kingdom of God. There are more than enough challenges, but the Church has in its possession a platform for dealing with those currents, which lead many to the edge of despair. The *Pastoral Constitution on the Church in the Modern World (Gaudium et Spes)* is that platform, and that platform is born of the Church's mission to be the agent of love in all things and at all times. Love, all love, is redemptive. Love with its basic components of forgiveness, acceptance, and compassion is always a divine gift and grace, no matter the gender of the persons involved.

The immediate challenge for my church is for it to support the creation and development of the awareness of Jesus's life and example of love. What if we abandon the guilt trips and get on board the forgiveness, real forgiveness, boat? What if we recognize in our actions that Jesus's love was for every person from the beginning of human life until the end of time—that the life of the convicted murderer on death row or of the terrorist suicide bomber is as precious to God as the life of the unborn? What if we mount a campaign that is aimed directly at opposing the culture of fear and its offspring—anger, deceit, fear, greed, and pride—and unveil them as the destroyers of soul and spirit?

Aquinas teaches us that daring is the child of hope, and that zest arises from the intensity of love. Hope leads us to see new vistas and releases us from the chains of what has always been done. It opens the door to change and conversion. Ours is a world where hope is not widespread; in fact, many are on the edge of despair and adopt a philosophy of "grab what you can because this is all that there is." So the question that must be faced as we think of evangelization, faith formation, or working to bring about the kingdom, is how do we create or educe hope? That is not just a question in the realm of faith; the troublesome issues of health care, school reform, and our aging population must also face that question. If we can grow hope, we can invite persons to have the courage to dream and the dare to change.

THOMAS W. MAHAN

Let me suggest that hope will not flourish until there is trust, and trust emerges from relationships. The late psychologist, Erik Erikson, pointed out that the first crisis of the newborn's existence is the discovery of how trustworthy the world is: Is she fed when hungry? Is she changed when uncomfortable? Is she cuddled when anxious? Those simple and basic actions create a climate where the infant develops an incipient sense of trust or mistrust. Those who are not fortunate enough to have the benefit of finding this early experience of life as trustworthy may spend a life continuing to test the world (people) on that dimension. For me, that means that the Church needs to rise up out of small groups where sharing can lead to exploring, then to discovery, and finally to making life choices. Neither large church assemblies nor lecture halls lend themselves to this intimate journey of exploring who I am, who God is, and discovering the avenues available for becoming a whole—and holy-person. Perhaps the model of the domestic church practiced in the early days of Christianity needs to be resurrected.

Still, there must be something that gives even a small group a sense of coherence and mission. Again, I suspect that the most immediately effective strategy to accomplish such coherence and purpose is threat. Just think of how the attack on Pearl Harbor in 1941 brought the country together. The same phenomenon was apparent after the terrorist attack on the Twin Towers in New York on 11 September 2001. Politicians seeking votes make good use of that strategy. The trouble with those examples is that they are built on fear, which leads to anger, retaliation, and the casting aside of the Jesus-message. Once the threat is gone, the coherence fades. Despite that fact, this negative approach is in rampant use in less dramatic forms in our political arena and, I regret to say, in some Church actions.

The alternative, born of the Jesus-message, is a vision, clearly articulated and passionately embraced by the leadership. In my mind, that vision is of the people of God, the church, shouting out the *new law*—the law of love—of acceptance of everybody, of openness. This new law shapes our way of being and acting; it moves out from home and family to the community and workplace. From there, it moves on to our political bodies and to the world in general. But at the heart of this process, there needs to be a small group where the members build trust that opens the door to sharing. That will take time and will require that each member is respected. In such a group, no position is rejected nor is any person put down for her ideas. Listening with an open mind and a caring heart is what ties the group together despite different perspectives or beliefs. In the mix of the sharing, new possibilities come to mind as the group explores what love means and how only love can bring us to joy. Together, the group members see themselves as becoming messengers of love in their daily lives as working to become passionate lovers. Is this a guaranteed result? Certainly not. Remember the Thomas Wolfe passage printed earlier in this document. He saw the light, he admired the call, he lacked the courage to follow through. Perhaps if he had been part of a supportive small group, things might have been different. We can neither deny nor avoid the fact that loving behavior can be demanding. Think again of our ultimate model of that behavior—Jesus.

Why is the Church not shouting out this vision of the law of love? Why is she not inviting all humanity to a crusade of loving one another? If evil, as Aquinas says, is the absence of the good, and evil in the human person is the absence of empathy, is not the crux of the pursuit of holiness the teaching and learning of empathy? Is not a supportive group where respect, listening, and sharing can lead to openness, freedom, and shedding of masks and fig leaves the best strategy for learning and practicing empathy? Is not the Mass, where we are called to celebrate joyfully the gift of divine love and life, the nourishment for our trust, hope, and love? Somehow, there seem to be only pockets of such activity in the Church of my experience. The problem, I suspect, is that we have been trapped in the culture of fear. As a result, we in the Church have often invested our energy into converting sinners through fear rather than rooting out sin through love. Even at a simpler level, how often do we hear of attendance at Sunday Mass as an obligation rather than a community love feast? For the observer, I wonder if the Church's image conveys a very mixed message. On the one hand, we are the earthly presence of Jesus, the incarnate, the divine passionate lover. On the other hand, we are the keeper of the keys to eternal happiness, so follow our rules or else. That double message does not sound like Jesus, the passionate lover, like the God of wild love and reckless giving.

There are two titles used down through the centuries to describe the office of the pope: the chief bridge builder (*pontifex maximus*) and the humblest of the servants of God (*servus servorum Dei*). The vision that I have been trying to set forth needs to have those titles take precedence over His Holiness, and similar images replace eminence for cardinals and excellency for bishops. Maybe all that is needed is to follow the monastic tradition where the abbot is often simply Father Francis. In the past half century, many diocesan clergy have encouraged being known as Father John rather than Father Murphy. When I was a youth, the use of such a title would have been seen as an insulting breach of respect. Now it conveys the unity of the clergy with the laity as lovers and members of the people of God.

Nonetheless, the paragraph above raises the question about the development process, formal and informal, that takes place in our seminaries. I have remarked on occasion that specific priests, usually recently ordained, seem to have mastered exceptionally well the course in Clerical Arrogance 101. (As I write that sentence, I am plagued by the thought that I too may have embraced the learnings of that course.) Leaving my frailties aside, the spirit of the preparation for ordination as a priest, an alter Christus, should reflect the role of bridge builder where his effort is to help all people join the crusade of love as well as the role of servant-leader, listening with caring ears both to the needs and to the ideas of the people of God and of those who have yet to sense the caring and compassion of the Church.

The *Catechism of the Catholic Church*, as mentioned earlier, has four parts, which have been summarized as follows: faith professed, faith expressed, faith lived, and faith prayed. At the heart of those four facets of our faith is the law of love, what I have been calling the Jesus-message.

Faith professed: we acknowledge the love of the Creator who gave us life and gave being to all that is; we wonder at the Teacher/Savior who took on the human condition to teach us how to live and love, who loved us to the giving of his life. We depend upon the Spirit present in us and in all creation and the God whose love is the grace that is everywhere.

Faith expressed: we come together as the people of God to celebrate and to be nourished, proclaiming by our presence that we believe and exult in the paschal mystery. We come to that enactment that we call the Mass to carry on a dialogue with the divine.

Faith lived: the faith that we have professed and expressed is empty if we do not embrace the Jesus-message and commit ourselves to testifying by our behavior to the dignity of every human person and show that commitment by love of all people. In 1 John 4:20-21, we read, "*If anyone says 'I love God,' but hates his brother, he is a liar; for whoever does not love a brother whom he has seen cannot love God whom he has not seen. This is the commandment that we have from him: whoever loves God must also love his brother.*"

Faith prayed: Aquinas tells us that "prayer is the expression of desire," and the basic desire that comes from our faith is the joy of loving and being loved. So our prayers are directed toward praise and thanksgiving, but with added petition for wisdom and fortitude. St. John Vianney (*the Cure D'Ars*) wrote that "it is always springtime in the heart that loves God." So our prayers will be overwhelmingly songs of delight and gratitude.

Actually, *enthusiasm for the faith* springs naturally from this perspective of the loving triune God who created us out of love, who became a human person to show us God's love and to call us to love all God's creatures, who is in us and around us, making grace available whenever and wherever we seek it. As I have suggested above, an outlook of trust and hope is the foundation for that faith, the foundation for a love that can shed conditions. Either consciously or subconsciously, each of us makes a choice to see the world around us permeated with either threat or potential. Either we will protect what we see as ours or we will open ourselves to new ventures. We will act from fear or from love and hope. Shakespeare caught the depths of the despair that can be the product of fear when he had Richard II say, "*Of comfort let no man speak. / Let's talk of graves and worms and epitaphs; / Make dust our paper, and with rainy eyes / Write sorrow on the bosom of the earth.*"

Contrast that with the words of Don Quixote sung in the stage production *The Man of La Mancha.* He sings, well aware of the negatives in the world: "*This is my quest to follow that star / No matter how hopeless, no matter how far / To fight for the right / Without question or pause, / To be willing to march into hell / For a heavenly cause!*"

Enthusiasm for the faith fills us with the spirit and the spirit for a joy-filled journey in the company of co-believers and co-adventurers who are the Church.

As I was preparing to send this manuscript to the publisher, I ran across a news article in my local newspaper, the *Asheville Citizen-Times.* It appeared on page 2 of the 25 October 2011 edition and was a report of a survey that is part of an ongoing research under the leadership of Catholic University sociology professor William D'Antonio. The summary of the results were intriguing. There was a table presenting the percentage of Catholic respondents who found eleven different Church teachings very important to them. At the top of the list (ranging from 73 percent agreement to 63 percent agreement) were four teachings: Jesus's resurrection, helping the poor, Mary as mother of God, and the Eucharist and other sacraments. The bottom four teachings where the percentage of the faithful calling them very important were, in descending order from 35 percent to 21 percent: opposition to same-sex marriage, accepting Vatican authority, opposition to the death penalty, and requiring celibate male clergy. In between were the following: daily prayer life (46 percent), opposition to abortion (40 percent), and devotions such as praying the rosary (36 percent).

THOMAS W. MAHAN

The cluster at the top is, to me, very good news; those beliefs that are central to the Jesus-message remain vibrant. Those at the bottom with the exception of "opposition to the death penalty" seem to reflect considerable rejection of the "power and control" orientation that I have found repulsive to many Catholics, practicing and lapsed. I also sense there are two interpretations that might be useful for the faithful to contemplate. First, we need to reemphasize what Joseph Cardinal Bernardin called the "seamless garment" when we speak of the preciousness of life and the dignity of the person, both themes of the Vatican II documents. In the survey report, we note the high ranking given to "helping the poor" in contrast to the mediocre stance on "opposition to abortion" (40 percent) and the very low position of "opposition to the death penalty" (29 percent). The poor are, of course, present in all our daily lives, so compassion for them comes more easily. Yet the commandment to love all people, to see Jesus in everybody does not let us off the hook because we volunteer at a homeless shelter or provide financial support for the starving in Africa. We, bishops, clergy, and laity, the people of God, are called to support all life, not just the poor or the unborn or the terminally ill, which means that we must be voices for universal health care, for full employment at a living wage, for adequate housing, and for universal quality education—at home and planet-wide.

The other inference that I draw from that survey is the sad chasm that seems to exist between the bishops (dare I say the magisterium?) and the faithful (dare I say the sensus fidelium?). My memory, fallible though it is, reminds me of how, after Blessed Pope John XXIII gave to the Church fathers the control of the council agenda, much overlap there seemed to be between the views of the council products and the people in the pews. It seemed that the lived experience of the faithful had become an important input into the expression of the Church's teachings. As Pope John XXIII sought out the thoughts and feelings of the assembled bishops rather than allow the curial cardinals to control the direction of the council, is it time for local bishops to recognize the dignity and talents of the faithful as they struggle to live the Jesus-message in the twenty-first-century world?

In a sense, this little volume has been asking, what do we human beings want? I suspect that our United States Declaration of Independence speaking of the "pursuit of happiness" certainly touches on a basic goal. Aquinas seems to agree with that when he said that humans all seek delight in one form or another. Freud, with a similar goal in mind, moves it clearly into the physical realm and calls it pleasure. We probably all can name for ourselves specific things or persons or images that are reasonably certain to give us happiness or delight or pleasure. What many of us would like is the assurance that there is a road open to us where we can achieve lasting delight or pleasure or happiness—I would suggest "joy" as the best term.

Yet many are reluctant to commit to suggested roads to that goal. In our modern world where change and uncertainty abound, many are in search of proof before commitment. No one, not even the Church, can provide us with the evidence such that we could say with certainty what is happening to our planet or what will happen to us after death. Certainty is a luxury that is a dream. What is reasonable is confidence. Confidence has to do with trust and hope; certainty depends upon evidence or incontrovertible deductive logic. Confidence is the proper measure of faith formation, and it gives the faith, leap, energy, and substance. As Aquinas wrote, "Faith does not quench desire; it inflames it."

And so I end this "love letter" to my church, to the people of God, and to its leaders. It is written as a gift, born of my wonder at the God of wild love and reckless giving. As my life moves inexorably toward its end, I am grateful for the wonder-filled life that I have had, and central to that gratitude is my awareness of how much my church has been the source of joy. I do not know whether this gift will be rejected, ignored, attacked, or maybe even embraced. But it remains my gift, and perhaps it too can be an occasion of grace. Grace is everywhere!

INDEX

A

abortion, 20–21, 37–38, 55, 70, 85, 90–91

acceptance, 26, 31–32, 34, 39, 41, 44, 49–50, 55–56, 61–63, 65–70, 72, 75, 85–86

Adam and Eve, 30, 33, 43, 50–52, 67, 78

anger, 27, 44, 54–56, 66, 68–69, 78, 85–87

Anselm of Canterbury, 25

Augustine, Saint, 25, 27–28, 30, 43, 84

B

Benedict XVI, Pope, 15

Bernanos, Georges, 24, 41, 65, 72, 74

Bernardin, Joseph Cardinal, 17, 34, 81, 91

C

Cameli, Louis J., 60

Catechism of the Catholic Church, 16, 20–21, 25, 28, 35–36, 68, 80, 89

Chesterton, G. K., 27

Christ-message, 31, 44

Code of Canon Law, 21, 35, 38, 47, 62, 72–73, 80–81

cohabitation, 22, 47–48

community, 24, 26, 30–31, 33, 42, 50, 58–61, 63, 65, 69–70, 72–73, 76, 79–80, 83, 87–88

compassion, 12, 19, 21, 31–34, 39, 41, 44, 49, 55–57, 59–63, 66–70, 72, 75–76, 79, 85–86

Constitution on the Sacred Liturgy, 41

contraception, 47

conversion, 31, 58, 63–65, 69, 79, 86

cross, 31, 58, 66, 68–69, 74

cultural war, 44

culture of fear, 24, 26–27, 30, 42, 44, 50–51, 55–56, 82–83, 85–86, 88

D

deceit, 19, 43, 51–56, 78, 82–83, 85–86

Declaration on Religious Liberty, 20

Diary of a Country Priest, 24, 41, 65, 74

Dogmatic Constitution on the Church, 45, 72

E

Eucharist, 20, 34, 38, 41, 70, 72, 79, 83, 90

F

faith, 11–12, 15–17, 23–24, 28–33, 37, 40, 47, 49, 51, 64, 67, 74, 78–86, 89–90, 92

N

Naked Now, The, 66
New Dictionary of Catholic Spirituality, 45, 50, 59
new law, 64, 83, 87
Nicene Creed, 29
nonviolence, 31, 58, 68–69

O

Olmsted, Thomas J., 55
O'Malley, John, SJ, 80–81
original sin, 30, 43, 67

P

Pastoral Constitution on the Church in the Modern World, 23, 82, 85–86
Paul, 30, 40–41, 43, 59, 65
Paul VI, Pope, 47, 82
Peck, M. Scott, 60
pride, 53–55, 63, 78, 85–86

R

Rohr, Richard, 12, 66

S

sacraments, 34, 55, 64, 72, 90
same-sex marriage, 49–50, 70, 90
sanctity, 45
sex, 19, 22, 45–47, 49, 52, 56
sin, 19, 23, 30, 33–35, 41–44, 46–47, 50–57, 63, 67, 70, 73, 88
suffering, 65–66, 68, 71, 74–75
Synod of Charleston, 80–81, 85

T

Teilhard de Chardin, Pierre, 37, 67
Thomas Aquinas, Saint, 24, 27–28, 35, 40, 42–43, 46, 51, 63, 68–69, 73, 77–79
Thompson, David B., Bishop, 12, 26, 63, 80–81, 85
Thompson, Francis, 26, 63

V

Vatican Council II, 37, 41

W

Wolfe, Thomas, 27, 29, 44, 63, 88

13874061R00055

Made in the USA
Lexington, KY
24 February 2012